Bond
No.1 for exam success

Non-verbal Reasoning

Assessment Papers

9–10 years

Book 2

OXFORD
UNIVERSITY PRESS

OXFORD
UNIVERSITY PRESS

Great Clarendon Street, Oxford, OX2 6DP, United Kingdom

Oxford University Press is a department of the University of Oxford.
It furthers the University's objective of excellence in research,
scholarship, and education by publishing worldwide. Oxford is
a registered trade mark of Oxford University Press in the UK and in
certain other countries

British Library Cataloguing in Publication Data
Data available

978-0-19-277742-3

10 9 8 7 6 5 4 3 2

Paper used in the production of this book is a natural, recyclable
product made from wood grown in sustainable forests.
The manufacturing process conforms to the environmental
regulations of the country of origin.

Printed in China

Acknowledgements

The publishers would like to thank the following for permissions to
use copyright material:

Page make-up: OKS Prepress, India
Illustrations: Bede Illustration
Cover illustrations: Lo Cole

Although we have made every effort to trace and contact all
copyright holders before publication this has not been possible in all
cases. If notified, the publisher will rectify any errors or omissions at
the earliest opportunity.

Links to third party websites are provided by Oxford in good faith
and for information only. Oxford disclaims any responsibility for
the materials contained in any third party website referenced in
this work.

What is Bond?

This book is part of the Bond Assessment Papers series for non-verbal reasoning, which provides a **thorough and progressive course in non-verbal reasoning** from ages six to twelve. It builds up non-verbal reasoning skills from book to book over the course of the series.

What does this book cover and how can it be used to prepare for exams?

Non-verbal reasoning questions can be grouped into four distinct groups: identifying shapes, missing shapes, rotating shapes, and coded shapes and logic. *Non-verbal Reasoning 9–10 years Book 1* and *Book 2* practise a wide range of questions appropriate to the age group drawn from all these categories. The papers can be used both for general practice and as part of the run-up to 11+ and other selective exams. One of the key features of Bond Assessment Papers is that each one practises **a very wide variety of skills and question types** so that children are always challenged to think – and don't get bored repeating the same question type again and again. We
believe that variety is the key to effective learning. It helps children 'think on their feet' and cope with the unexpected: it is surprising how often children come out of non-verbal reasoning exams having met question types they have not seen before.

What does the book contain?

- **6 papers** – each one contains 54 questions.
- **Tutorial links throughout –** [book icon] – this icon appears next to the questions. It indicates links to the relevant section in *How to do 11+ Non-verbal Reasoning*, our invaluable subject guide that offers explanations and practice for all core question types.
- **Scoring devices** – there are score boxes at the end of each paper and a Progress Chart on page 56. The chart is a visual and motivating way for children to see how they are doing. It also turns the score into a percentage that can help decide what to do next.
- **Next Steps Planner** – advice on what to do after finishing the papers can be found on the inside back cover.
- **Answers** – located in an easily-removed central pull-out section.

How can you use this book?

One of the great strengths of Bond Assessment Papers is their flexibility. They can be used at home, in school and by tutors to:

- set **timed formal practice** tests – allow about 40 minutes per paper. Reduce the suggested time limit by five minutes to practise working at speed.

- provide **bite-sized chunks** for regular practice
- **highlight strengths and weaknesses** in the core skills
- identify **individual needs**
- set **homework**
- follow a **complete 11⁺ preparation strategy** alongside *The Parents' Guide to the 11⁺* (see below).

It is best to start at the beginning and work through the papers in order. If you are using the book as part of a careful run-in to the 11⁺, we suggest that you also have two other essential Bond resources close at hand:

How to do 11⁺ Non-verbal Reasoning: the subject guide that explains all the question types practised in this book. Use the cross-reference icons to find the relevant sections.

The Parents' Guide to the 11⁺: the step-by-step guide to the whole 11⁺ experience. It clearly explains the 11⁺ process, provides guidance on how to assess children, helps you to set complete action plans for practice and explains how you can use *Non-verbal Reasoning 9–10 years Book 1* and *Book 2* as part of a strategic run-in to the exam.

See the inside front cover for more details of these books.

What does a score mean and how can it be improved?

It is unfortunately impossible to predict how a child will perform when it comes to the 11⁺ (or similar) exam if they achieve a certain score on any practice book or paper. Success on the day depends on a host of factors, including the scores of the other children sitting the test. However, we can give some guidance on what a score indicates and how to improve it.

If children colour in the Progress Chart on page 56, this will give an idea of present performance in percentage terms. The Next Steps Planner inside the back cover will help you to decide what to do next to help a child progress. It is always valuable to go over wrong answers with children. If they are having trouble with any particular question type, follow the tutorial links to *How to do 11⁺ Non-verbal Reasoning* for step-by-step explanations and further practice.

Don't forget the website . . . !

Visit www.bond11plus.co.uk for lots of advice, information and suggestions on everything to do with Bond, the 11⁺ and helping children to do their best.

Paper 1

Which is the odd one out? Circle the letter.

Example

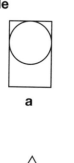

a   b   ⓒ   d   e

1

a   b   c   d   e

2

a   b   c   d   e

3

a   b   c   d   e

4

a   b   c   d   e

5

a   b   c   d   e

6

a   b   c   d   e

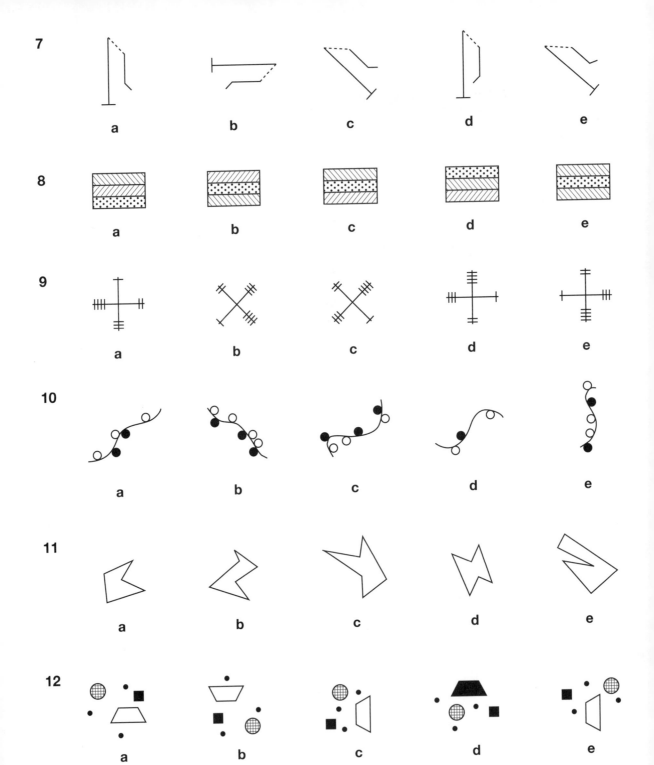

7 a b c d e

8 a b c d e

9 a b c d e

10 a b c d e

11 a b c d e

12 a b c d e

B 4   Which one comes next? Circle the letter.

Example

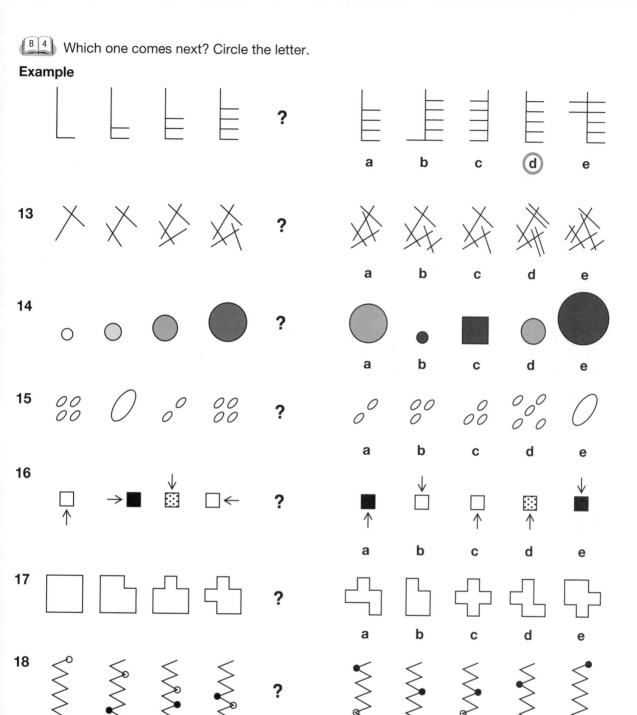

13

14

15

16

17

18

19

3

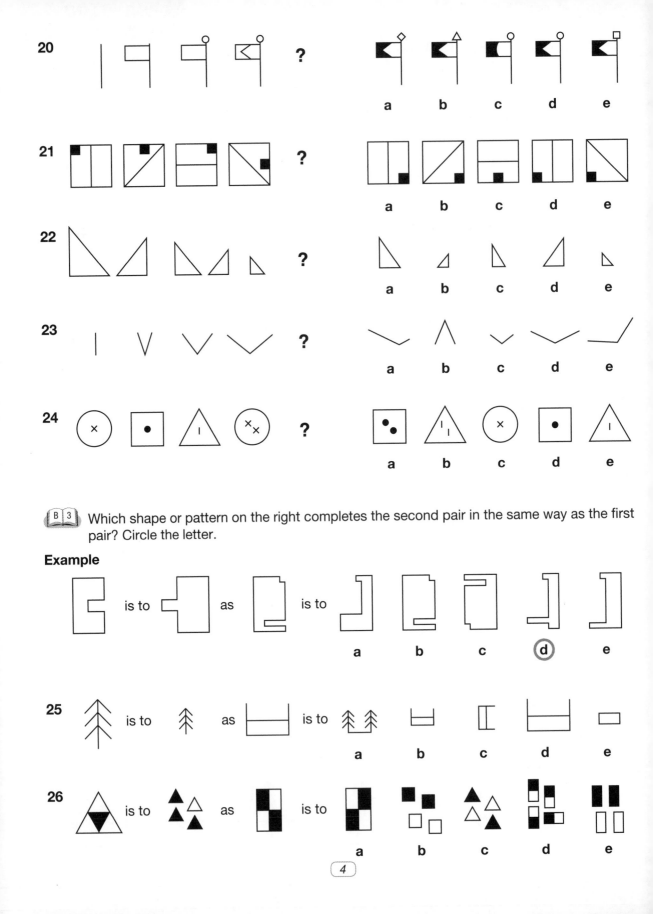

20

21

22

23

24

B 3 Which shape or pattern on the right completes the second pair in the same way as the first pair? Circle the letter.

Example

is to ___ as ___ is to

a   b   c   d   e

25 is to ___ as ___ is to

a   b   c   d   e

26 is to ___ as ___ is to

a   b   c   d   e

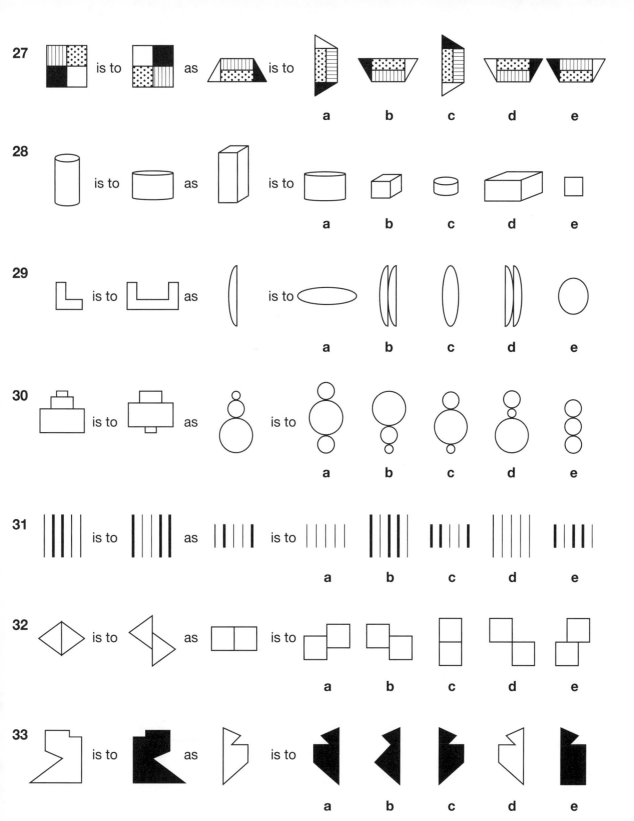

27 is to ... as ... is to
    a   b   c   d   e

28 is to ... as ... is to
    a   b   c   d   e

29 is to ... as ... is to
    a   b   c   d   e

30 is to ... as ... is to
    a   b   c   d   e

31 is to ... as ... is to
    a   b   c   d   e

32 is to ... as ... is to
    a   b   c   d   e

33 is to ... as ... is to
    a   b   c   d   e

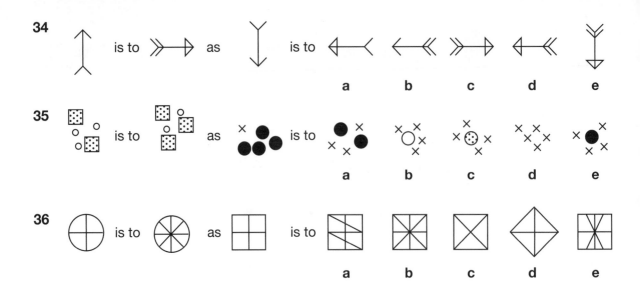

34

35

36

In which larger shape is the shape on the left hidden? Circle the letter.

Example

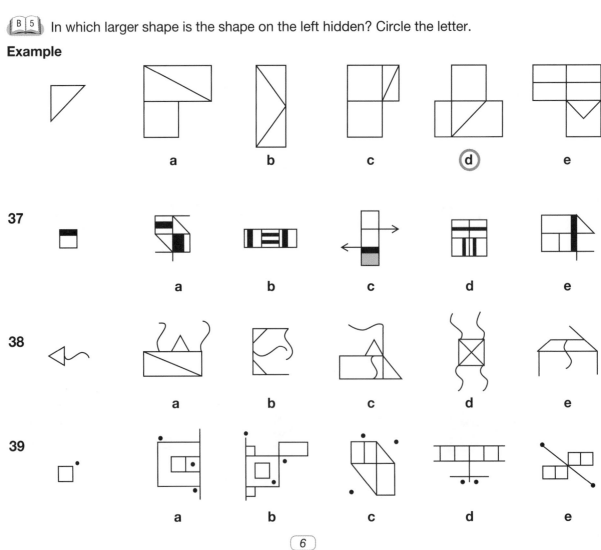

a   b   c   (d)   e

37

a   b   c   d   e

38

a   b   c   d   e

39

a   b   c   d   e

40

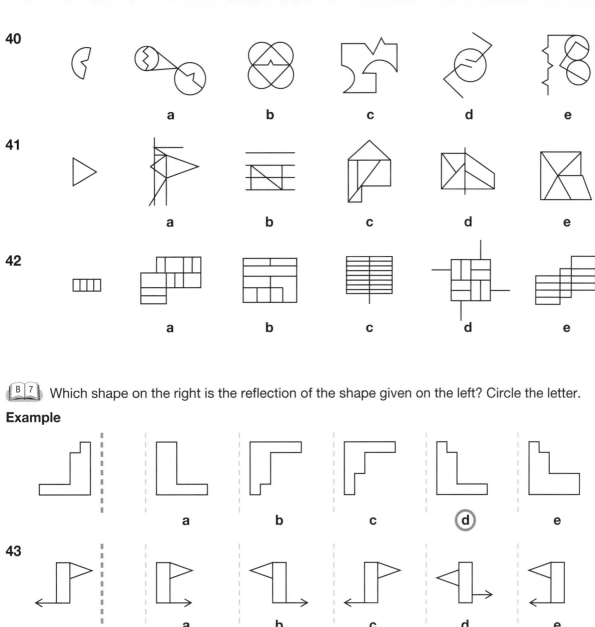

a   b   c   d   e

41

a   b   c   d   e

42

a   b   c   d   e

[B 7] Which shape on the right is the reflection of the shape given on the left? Circle the letter.

Example

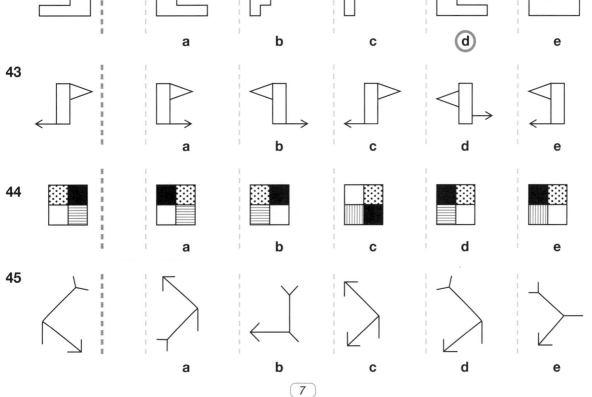

a   b   c   (d)   e

43

a   b   c   d   e

44

a   b   c   d   e

45

a   b   c   d   e

46

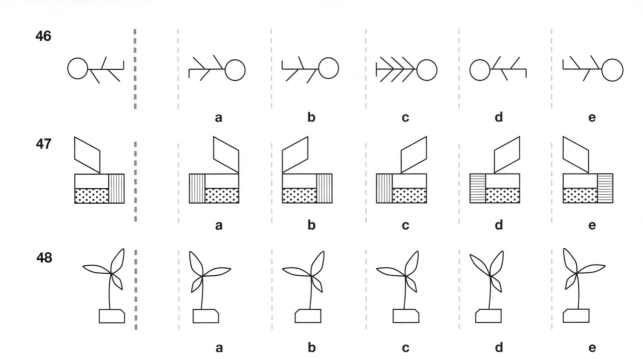

| | a | b | c | d | e |

47

| a | b | c | d | e |

48

| a | b | c | d | e |

B 9   Which code matches the shape or pattern given at the end of each line? Circle the letter.

Example

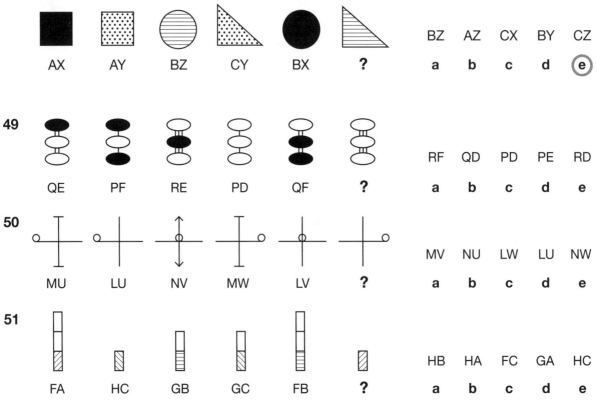

| | | | | | | BZ | AZ | CX | BY | CZ |
| AX | AY | BZ | CY | BX | ? | a | b | c | d | (e) |

49

| | | | | | | RF | QD | PD | PE | RD |
| QE | PF | RE | PD | QF | ? | a | b | c | d | e |

50

| | | | | | | MV | NU | LW | LU | NW |
| MU | LU | NV | MW | LV | ? | a | b | c | d | e |

51

| | | | | | | HB | HA | FC | GA | HC |
| FA | HC | GB | GC | FB | ? | a | b | c | d | e |

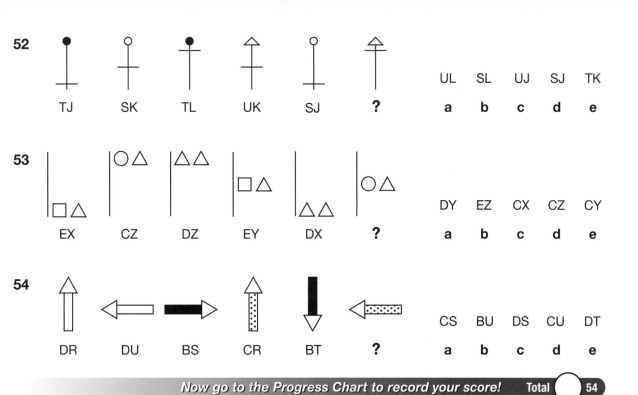

52

TJ   SK   TL   UK   SJ   ?

	UL	SL	UJ	SJ	TK
	a	b	c	d	e

53

EX   CZ   DZ   EY   DX   ?

	DY	EZ	CX	CZ	CY
	a	b	c	d	e

54

DR   DU   BS   CR   BT   ?

	CS	BU	DS	CU	DT
	a	b	c	d	e

Now go to the Progress Chart to record your score!   Total ◯ 54

Paper 2

B 1 Which is the odd one out? Circle the letter.

Example

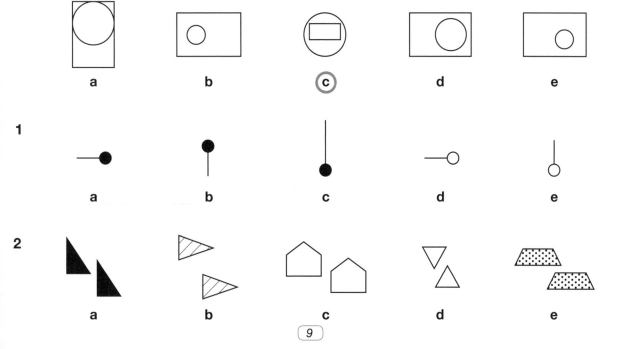

a   b   c   d   e

1

a   b   c   d   e

2

a   b   c   d   e

9

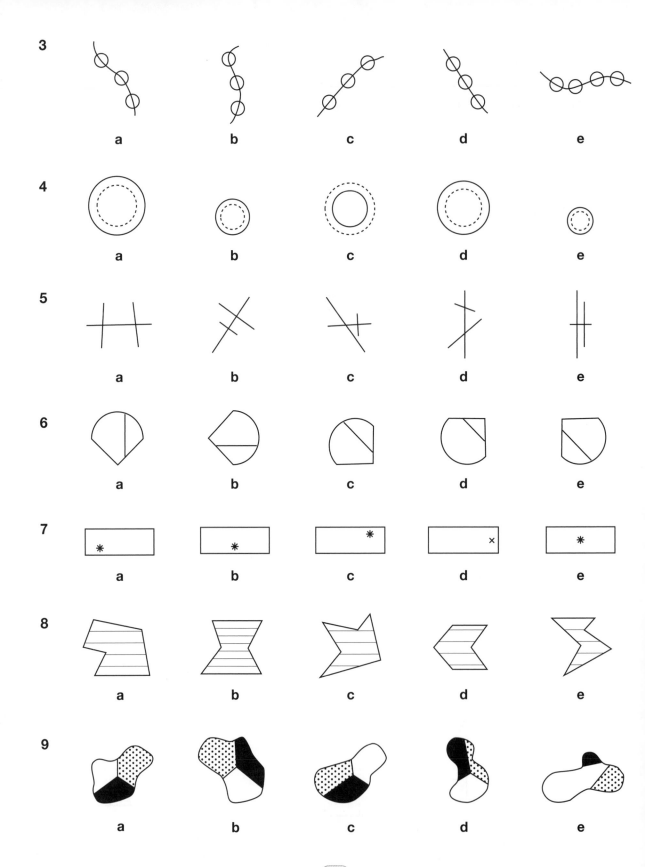

10

a   b   c   d   e

11

a   b   c   d   e

12

a   b   c   d   e

B 4 Which one comes next? Circle the letter.

Example

?   a   b   c   (d)   e

13

?   a   b   c   d   e

14

?   a   b   c   d   e

15

?   a   b   c   d   e

16

?   a   b   c   d   e

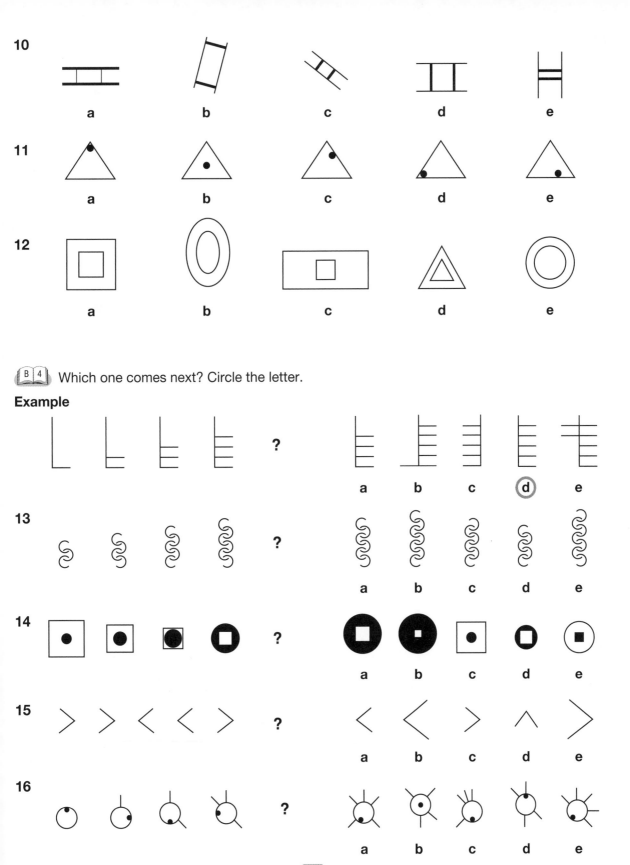

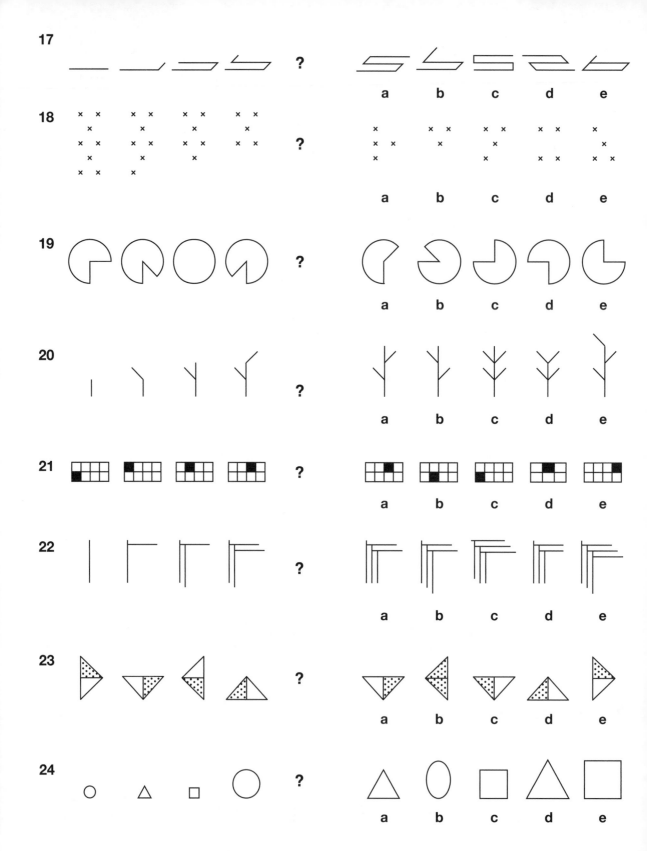

17

a   b   c   d   e

18

a   b   c   d   e

19

a   b   c   d   e

20

a   b   c   d   e

21

a   b   c   d   e

22

a   b   c   d   e

23

a   b   c   d   e

24

a   b   c   d   e

B 3 Which shape or pattern on the right completes the second pair in the same way as the first pair? Circle the letter.

Example

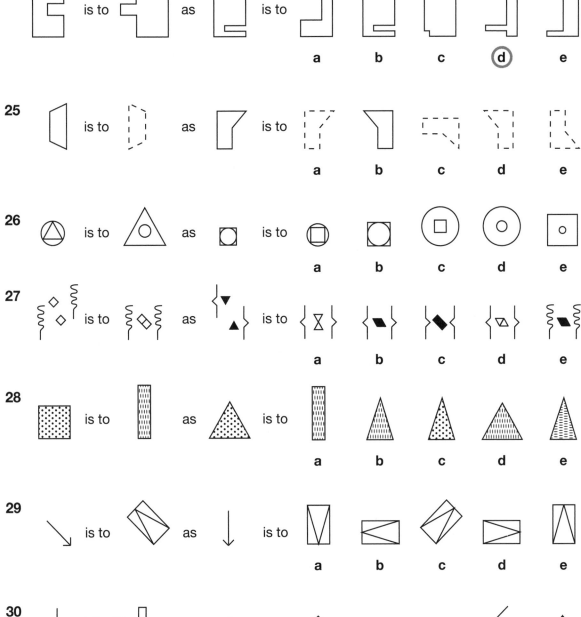

25

26

27

28

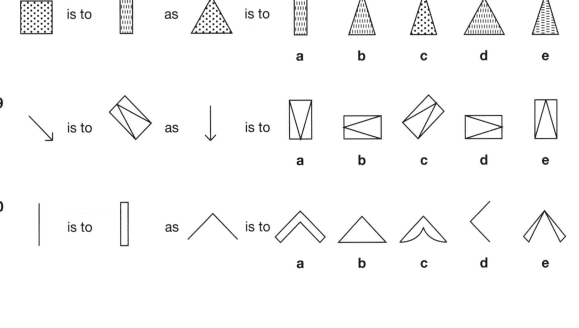

29

30

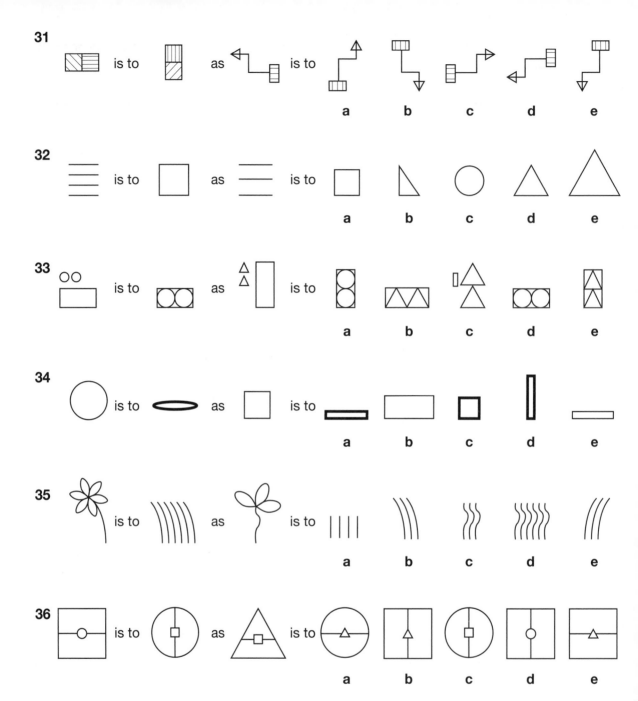

31

32

33

34

35

36

a   b   c   d   e

In which larger shape is the shape on the left hidden? Circle the letter.

Example

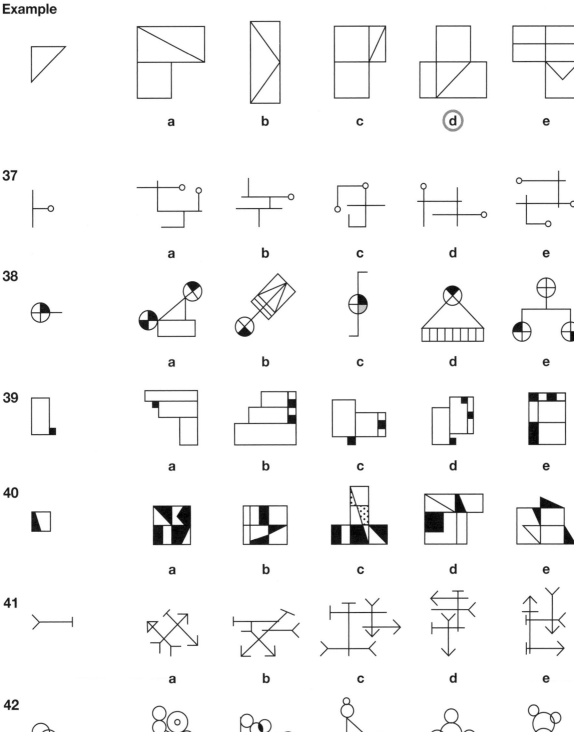

a   b   c   (d)   e

37

a   b   c   d   e

38

a   b   c   d   e

39

a   b   c   d   e

40

a   b   c   d   e

41

a   b   c   d   e

42

a   b   c   d   e

Which shape on the right is the reflection of the shape given on the left? Circle the letter.

Example

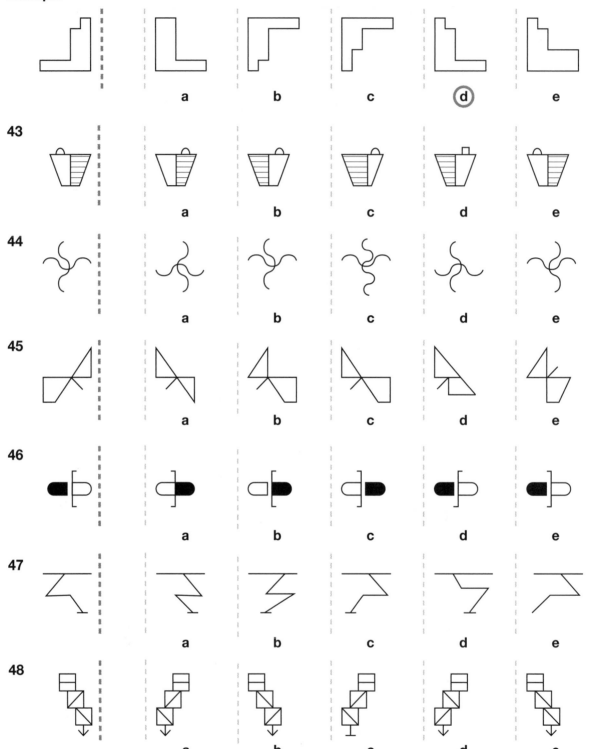

a b c d e

43

a b c d e

44

a b c d e

45

a b c d e

46

a b c d e

47

a b c d e

48

a b c d e

B 6 Which shape or pattern completes the larger square? Circle the letter.

Example

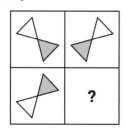   

a   b   c   (d)   e

49

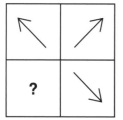

a   b   c   d   e

50

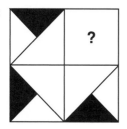

a   b   c   d   e

51

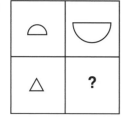

a   b   c   d   e

52

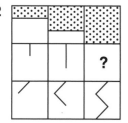

a   b   c   d   e

53

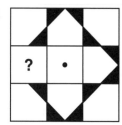

a   b   c   d   e

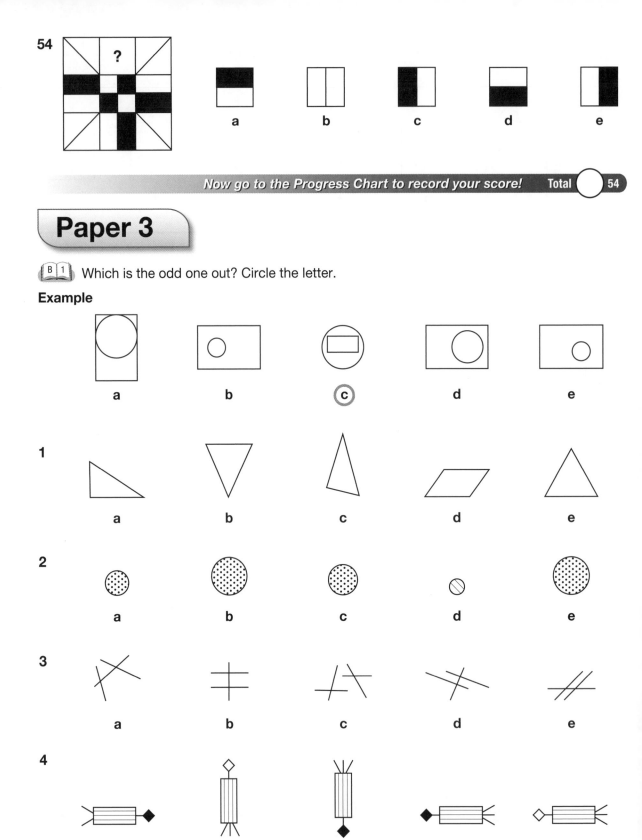

54

Now go to the Progress Chart to record your score! Total ◯ 54

Paper 3

B 1 Which is the odd one out? Circle the letter.

Example

a b c d e

1 a b c d e

2 a b c d e

3 a b c d e

4 a b c d e

18

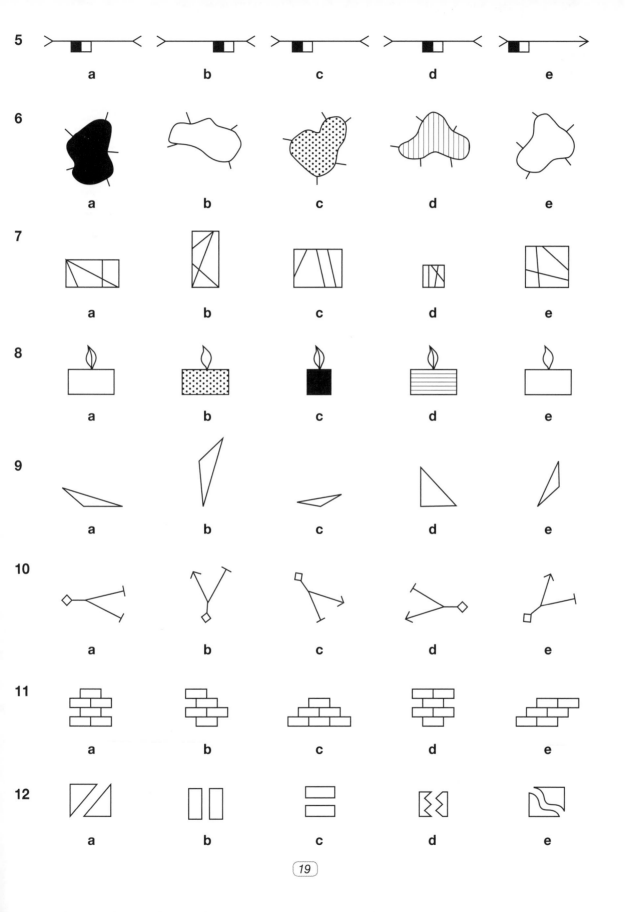

5

    a   b   c   d   e

6

    a   b   c   d   e

7

    a   b   c   d   e

8

    a   b   c   d   e

9

    a   b   c   d   e

10

    a   b   c   d   e

11

    a   b   c   d   e

12

    a   b   c   d   e

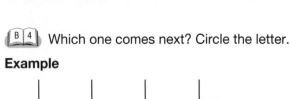 Which one comes next? Circle the letter.

Example

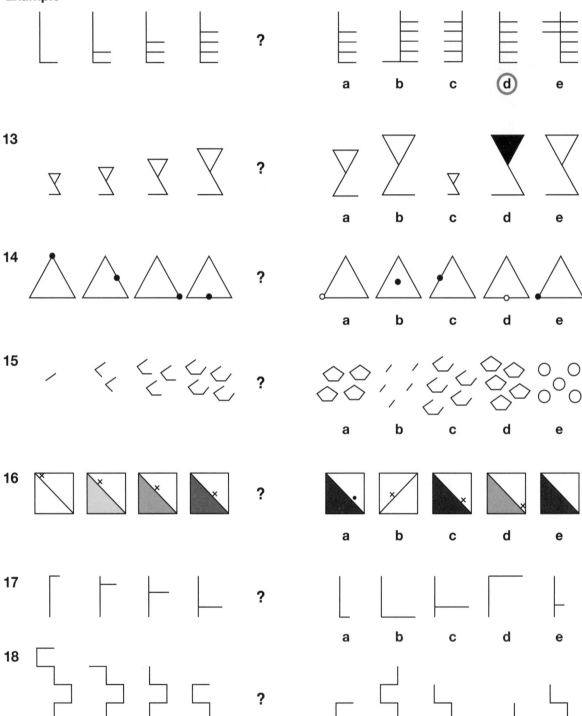

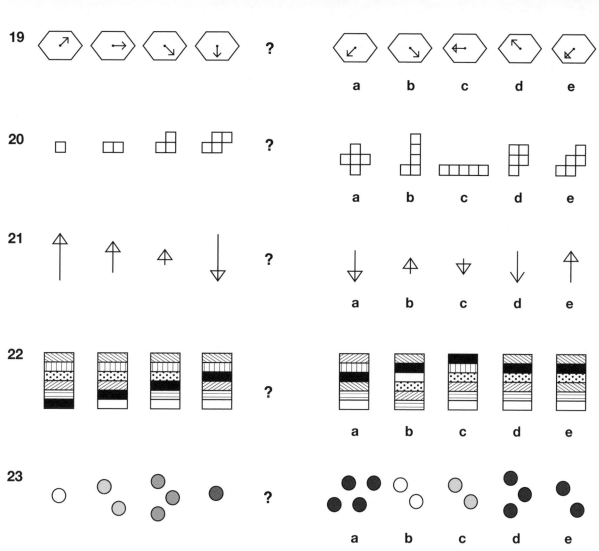

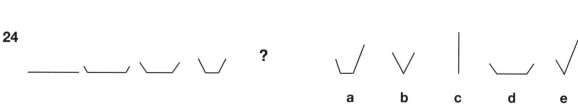

Which shape or pattern on the right completes the second pair in the same way as the first pair? Circle the letter.

Example

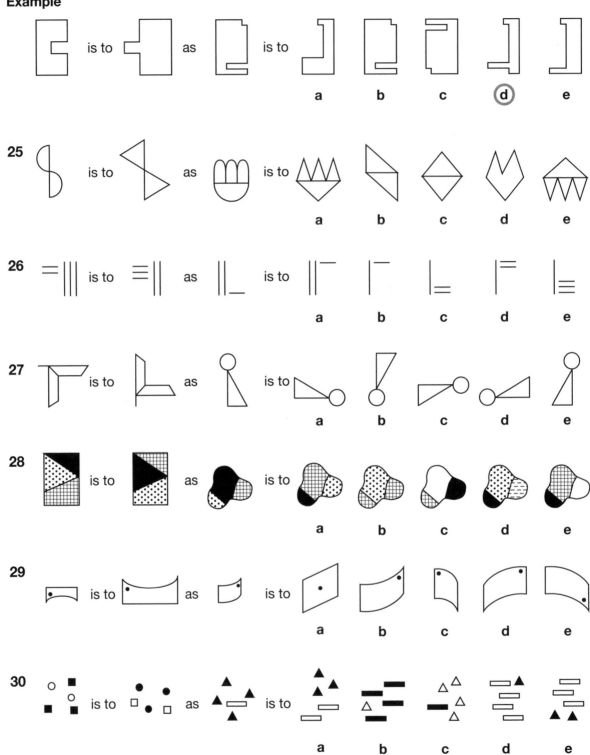

25

26

27

28

29

30

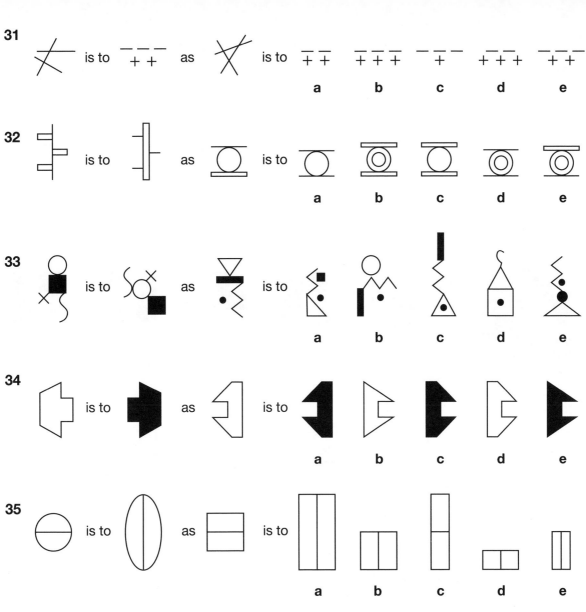

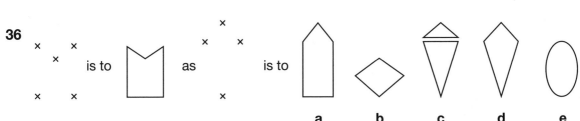

B 6 Which shape or pattern completes the larger square? Circle the letter.

Example

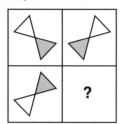

                                        a   b   c   (d)   e

37

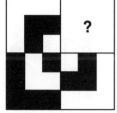

                                          a   b   c   d   e

38

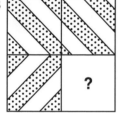

                                          a   b   c   d   e

39

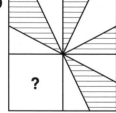

                                          a   b   c   d   e

40

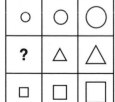

                                          a   b   c   d   e

5 **a** All of the options, apart from a, are made up of three lines of different length (short, medium and long).

6 **d** All of the shapes, apart from d, have a line through the shape in the same place.

7 **d** All of the rectangles, apart from d, contain the same shape.

8 **b** All of the shapes, apart from b, have the same distance between the horizontal stripes.

9 **e** All of the shapes, apart from e, have the black and spotted sections touching one another.

10 **a** All of the shapes apart from a have two long, thin lines with two short, thick lines perpendicular between them.

11 **b** All of the shapes apart from b have a black circle touching one or more sides of a triangle.

12 **c** All of the shapes apart from c are made up of one smaller shape with an enlargement of that shape around it.

13 **b** The pattern has one new curved section each time. The top curved section is always open to the right which means the bottom curved section alternates between being open to the left and open to the right.

14 **b** The white square decreases in size while the black circle increases in size.

15 **c** The sequence has two right-hand chevrons, two left-hand chevrons and then two right-hand chevrons, all of the same size.

16 **d** The small black circle moves clockwise around the larger white circle 90° each time. The quantity of small black lines increases by one each time.

17 **a** The pattern has one new line added each time to continue the "snaking" shape going up the page.

18 **c** One cross is removed each time, working right to left, then upwards, through the arrangement of crosses.

19 **d** One eighth is added to the circle each time in a clockwise direction until it becomes whole again, then one eighth is removed each time.

20 **a** The pattern alternates between a vertical line being added and a diagonal line being added.

21 **e** The small black square moves around the rectangle one small white square at a time, in a clockwise direction.

22 **b** The pattern alternates between a short vertical line being added and a longer horizontal line being added. The horizontal lines are all the same length as each other. The vertical lines are all the same length as each other but longer than the horizontal lines.

23 **e** The shape rotates 90° clockwise each time.

24 **a** The pattern is small circle, small triangle, small square followed by the same shapes in the same order but slightly larger in size.

25 **d** The second shape is a vertical reflection of the first shape, with the solid line changed to a dashed line.

26 **c** In the second image, the inner and outer shapes are swapped and they no longer touch.

27 **b** In the second image, the four separate shapes are moved up or down to meet in the middle.

28 **b** The second shape is a taller, thinner version of the first shape and the shading is changed from spots to short vertical lines.

29 **e** In the second shape, the rectangle is positioned at the same angle as the arrow in the first shape. The two diagonal lines within the rectangle make a point in the opposite direction to the arrow head.

30 **a** The second shape is a thicker version of the first shape.

31 **e** The second shape is a 90° anticlockwise rotation of the first shape.

32 **d** The second shape is made up of the lines in the first shape. The length of the lines remain the same.

33 **e** The second image has the two small shapes from the first image put inside the rectangle and enlarged to fill the space. The rectangle remains unchanged.

34 **a** The second shape is the first shape squashed vertically with a thicker line.

35 **c** Each shape in the second image is the same shape as the "stem" from the first image. The number of shapes in the second image is the same as the number of "petals" in the first image.

36 **b** In the second image the inner and outer shapes from the first image are swapped and the horizontal line becomes a vertical line.

37 **c**

38 **e**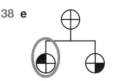

39 **d**

Bond Non-Verbal Reasoning Assessment Papers 9–10 years Book 2

40 b

41 e

42 c

43–48 When each shape is paired with the correct reflection, they form a single shape that is perfectly symmetrical.

43 b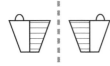

44 e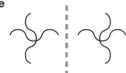

45 c

46 c

47 c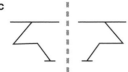

48 d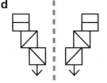

49 a The missing square is a 90° clockwise rotation of the bottom right square.

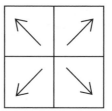

50 b The missing square is a 90° clockwise rotation of the top left square.

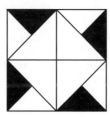

51 c The missing square contains the same shape as the bottom left square, reflected horizontally and enlarged.

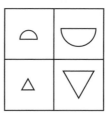

52 e The shape or pattern in each row enlarges each time, from left to right, so the line touches the top and bottom of the square.

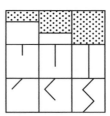

53 d The missing square is a vertical reflection of the middle right square.

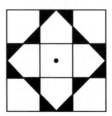

54 **c** The missing square is a 180° rotation of the bottom middle square.

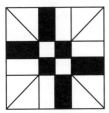

Paper 3 (pages 18–27)

1 **d** All of the shapes, apart from d, are triangles.
2 **d** All of the shapes, apart from d, are circles with a spotted pattern.
3 **c** All of the shapes, apart from c, have three lines.
4 **a** All of the shapes, apart from a, have three short lines at one end of the rectangle.
5 **e** All of the shapes, apart from e, have matching short lines at both ends of the long horizontal line.
6 **b** All of the shapes, apart from b, have five short lines around the edge of the shape.
7 **c** All of the shapes, apart from c, have two of the lines inside the rectangle crossing over each other.
8 **c** All of the shapes, apart from c, have a rectangle with two longer and two shorter sides.
9 **d** All of the shapes, apart from d, are triangles with an obtuse angle.
10 **a** All of the shapes, apart from a, have a square, a straight line and an arrow head at the end of the lines.
11 **b** All of the shapes, apart from b, have six identical rectangles.
12 **b** All of the shapes, apart from b, form a square when the two parts are put together.
13 **e** The shape continues to get bigger.
14 **e** The black circle moves clockwise around the triangle, alternating between stopping on a corner and halfway along a side.
15 **d** One line is added to the shape each time and the number of shapes is the same as the number of lines used to create each shape.
16 **c** The triangle shading gradually gets darker and the x moves down the diagonal line.
17 **b** The horizontal line gets slightly longer each time while moving down the vertical line.
18 **c** The number of lines making up the shape reduces by one each time.
19 **a** The arrow moves clockwise around the hexagon, 45° each time. The arrowhead remains the same throughout.

20 **e** One square is added each time, alternating between being added to the right of, or above, the previously added square.
21 **a** The arrow length shortens each time, then changes direction and returns to full length. It then gradually shortens each time again.
22 **d** The rectangle that is shaded black moves up one each time. The patterns in the rest of the rectangles remain in the same place.
23 **e** The sequence is formed of one, then two, then three circles before returning to one and so on. The shading gradually gets darker.
24 **b** The sides bend up more each time, always keeping the shape symmetrical.
25 **a** The second shape has points in place of curves.
26 **c** The second shape has the opposite number of horizontal and vertical lines to the first shape. The lines remain in the same positions.
27 **d** The second shape is a 90° anticlockwise rotation of the first shape.
28 **a** In the second shape, the black shading becomes a cross-hatched pattern, the spotted pattern becomes black and the cross-hatched pattern becomes spotted.
29 **e** The second shape is the first shape enlarged and reflected horizontally.
30 **b** In the second image, the quantity and colour of the shapes in the first image is swapped.
31 **b** The second image shows the number of lines from the first image and uses + symbols to show the number of times those lines crossed.
32 **e** In the second image, the thin lines become thicker and the thick lines become thin ones.
33 **c** The second image is made up of exactly the same shapes as in the first image but arranged differently.
34 **c** The second shape is a vertical reflection of the first shape, coloured black.
35 **a** The second shape is the first shape elongated vertically and with the horizontal line swapped to a vertical line.
36 **d** The second shape is made by drawing a line between the crosses in the first shape.
37 **b** The missing square is a diagonal reflection of the bottom left square.

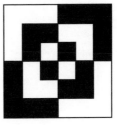

EXPANDED ANSWERS

Bond Non-Verbal Reasoning Assessment Papers 9–10 years Book 2

38 **c** The missing square is a horizontal reflection of the top right square.

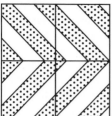

39 **b** The missing square is a diagonal reflection of the top right square. The lines in the shapes remain horizontal.

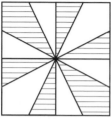

40 **e** Each row shows a shape that gradually increases in size from left to right.

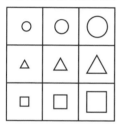

41 **a** As in the top and middle rows, the missing square in the right-hand column matches the square in the bottom left-hand column.

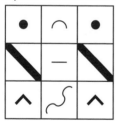

42 **a** The missing square is a horizontal reflection of the top middle square.

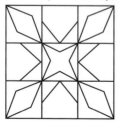

43 **d** The first letter represents the position of the small shape within the large white square

(F has the small shape in the bottom right corner, G has it at the bottom and in the middle and H has it in the middle of the square). The second letter represents the small shape within the large white square (V has a circle, W has a triangle and X has a square).

44 **d** The first letter represents the bottom half of the shape (A has a single vertical line, B has a chevron and C has a vertical line joined to a chevron). The second letter represents the shape and direction of the arrow in the top half of the shape (J has a straight arrow pointing right, K has a curved arrow pointing right and L has a curved arrow pointing left).

45 **c** The first letter represents the size of the triangle (R has a small triangle, S has a medium triangle and T has a large triangle). The second letter represents the orientation of the triangle (M has the triangle pointing up, N has it pointing right and O has it pointing down).

46 **a** The first letter represents the number of sides of the shape (C has three sides, D has four sides and E has five sides). The second letter represents the type of shading (P has no shading, Q has horizontal lines and R has vertical lines).

47 **e** The first letter represents the overall shape and orientation (T has a rectangle, U has a curve at the top and V has a curve at the bottom). The second letter represents what is inside the overall shape (L has nothing, M has a triangle pointing upwards and N has a triangle pointing downwards).

48 **a** The first letter represents the thickness of the main shape (H has a thick shape, I has a thin shape and J has a single line). The second letter represents the number of lines at the bottom of the shape (E has three lines, F has two lines and G has one line).

49 **d**

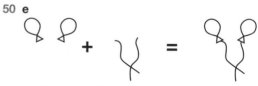

The square is joined to the top of the longer line.

50 **e**

The "balloons" line up on top of the "strings".

51 **c**

The second shape is aligned with the left-hand and bottom sections of the first shape, overlapping it.

52 b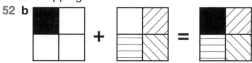

The two larger squares line up on top of each other with the white square in the second shape being replaced with the black square of the first shape.

53 c

Both shapes are rotated 90° clockwise. The second shape is then placed inside the first shape.

54 a

Both shapes are rotated 180° clockwise. The white triangle is aligned with the black triangle.

Paper 4 (pages 27–36)

1 **d** All of the shapes, apart from d, are made up of one vertical and two horizontal lines.

2 **c** All of the shapes, apart from c, have a dashed line of symmetry.

3 **a** All of the shapes, apart from a, have two short lines that point in opposite directions.

4 **e** All of the shapes, apart from e, are made up of four lines, each one a different length.

5 **a** All of the shapes, apart from a, have a square with diagonal lines that slope downwards to the right.

6 **b** All of the shapes, apart from b, are made up of five lines of equal length.

7 **b** All of the shapes, apart from b, have a black shaded triangle or square in them.

8 **d** All of the shapes, apart from d, have a triangle or semi-circle at the top of the rectangle.

9 **b** All of the shapes, apart from b, are made up of two equal length lines.

10 **e** All of the shapes, apart from e, have a triangular shaded overlap.

11 **c** All of the shapes, apart from c, have a middle line that is the same length.

12 **a** All of the shapes, apart from a, have three x symbols.

13 **b** The lowest small square is removed each time. The horizontal line moves down the rectangle each time.

14 **c** There are three elements to this sequence: the shapes alternate between a square and triangle; the pattern is a sequence of white, black, then striped; and two shapes are the same size before getting bigger.

15 **c** The shapes in the sequence have one less side each time.

16 **d** The circle at the beginning of the sequence is gradually stretched, getting taller and thinner.

17 **a** The sequence is of a shape that is reflected vertically, then reflected horizontally and so on.

18 **d** An extra short line is added to the centre of the circle in a clockwise direction until it reaches three, then it returns to one. The small black circle moves clockwise around the circumference of the circle, one quarter at a time.

19 **c** The small white square moves to the right and the bottom horizontal line is removed each time.

20 **e** The shading darkens each time.

21 **e** An alternating sequence in which a horizontal line of increasing length is added at the bottom of the shape followed by a short vertical line at the bottom of the shape.

22 **b** One extra square containing a black dot is added to the bottom each time. One diagonal line is also added, in a clockwise direction, to each square.

23 **e** One side of a triangle is added each time, moving anticlockwise, first with a solid line and then with a dashed line.

24 **a** One of the diagonal lines moves down the vertical line each time, alternating between the line on the left and the line on the right.

25 **a** The second shape is made by putting the individual pieces from the first shape together and changing the colour. White becomes black, black becomes grey and grey becomes white.

26 **c** The number of thin black lines is doubled. The thick black line remains unchanged.

27 **d** In the second shape, the shapes and sizes are reversed. Each shape retains its shading/colour.

28 **b** In the second shape, the wavy lines are joined together at the top and the single shape is added to the bottom of each line.

29 **c** In the second shape, the size of the outer shape has been reduced and the x changed to an enlarged +.

30 **e** The second shape is the first shape stretched vertically, to a similar size to the one shown in the example.

31 **b** The second shape is made by putting the two pieces from the first shape together and then adding a second, identical copy of the shape next to the original.

32 **c** The second shape is a vertical reflection of the first shape with the shading reversed (black becomes white and white becomes black).

33 **d** In the second shape, thin black lines become thick black lines and thick black lines become thin black lines.

34 **d** In the second shape, the smaller shapes move to the nearest outer corners of the larger shape and the shading in the smaller shapes is reversed (black becomes white and white becomes black).

35 **e** In the second shape the width of the two parts of the arrow swap over.

36 **b** The second shape is the first shape stretched diagonally. The inner line remains unchanged.

37 **a**

38 **d**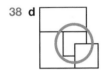

39 **c**

40 **c**

41 **d**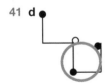

42 **b**

43 **c** The missing square has a large version of the small shape in the right-hand square and the lines are removed, so it will be large white square positioned diagonally.

44 **b** The missing square is a horizontal reflection of the bottom left-hand square.

45 **e** Moving down each column, a new line or shape is added each time, which gradually decreases in size.

46 **b** Each row shows a dot that moves to alternate sides of the line, so the missing square will have a black dot on the opposite side of the diagonal line to the other two in the same row.

47 **c** The missing square is a vertical reflection of the small square to the left.

48 **a** The missing square is a 90° clockwise rotation of the small square to the right.

49 **e**

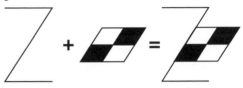

The two shapes are moved horizontally towards each other and joined without any other changes.

50 **b**

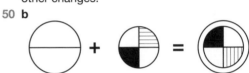

The larger circle is rotated 90° in either direction. The second, smaller circle, is rotated 90° clockwise and overlaps the larger circle.

51 **a**

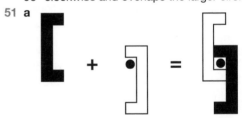

The two shapes are moved horizontally towards each other and then rotated 180°.

52 **d**

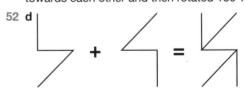

The two shapes are moved horizontally towards each other, overlapping one another, and joined without any other changes.

53 **e**

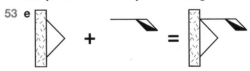

The two shapes are moved horizontally towards each other and joined without any other changes.

A8

54 **c**

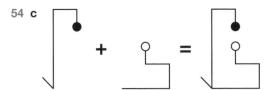

The two shapes are moved horizontally towards each other and joined without any other changes.

Paper 5 (pages 37–45)

1 **a** All of the shapes, apart from a, have four small squares shaded with diagonal lines.
2 **d** All of the shapes, apart from d, are triangles.
3 **c** All of the shapes, apart from, c have a triangle that is larger than the circle.
4 **b** All of the shapes, apart from b, have a solid black line.
5 **c** All of the shapes, apart from c, have a short horizontal line.
6 **e** All of the shapes, apart from e, have two short lines pointing towards each other.
7 **e** All of the shapes, apart from e, are made up of four identical parts.
8 **b** All of the shapes, apart from b, have a long line the same length and the larger triangle at the very end of the line.
9 **d** All of the shapes, apart from d, have exactly half shaded (excluding the "neck" part of the bottle).
10 **a** All of the shapes, apart from a, all have short diagonal lines pointing in the same direction.
11 **c** All of the shapes, apart from c, have a "T" shape in the middle.
12 **d** All of the shapes, apart from d, are quadrilaterals.
13 **a** The line moves 90° clockwise and one extra line is added each time to turn it into an arrow.
14 **b** The sequence is three large shapes (circle, square, triangle), which then repeats with smaller shapes. The shading alternates between horizontal lines and white.
15 **e** The short line moves about 30° clockwise each time.
16 **d** A solid line is added and a reflection of this is added to the dotted line on the next image in the sequence.
17 **a** One small square is added each time.
18 **a** The line has one less loop each time.
19 **e** One small black circle is added each time. The outer shapes remain the same.
20 **c** A solid line is added each time in an anticlockwise direction. The lines that are already shown in the shape alternate between a solid line and a dashed line each time.

21 **b** The shape rotates 90° anticlockwise each time. The line shading in one section is always horizontal.
22 **b** Each line forming the circle gets cut in half each time.
23 **e** The shape reduces in size each time. The shape and orientation remain the same.
24 **c** The short, thick black line moves 45° clockwise around the centre of the long, thin black line each time.
25 **b** In the second image the number of small shapes inside the large outer shape matches the number of shapes or lines around the outside of the large outer shape in the first image.
26 **a** In the second shape the shading in the first shape is swapped so black becomes striped and striped becomes black.
27 **d** The second shape is an enlarged version of the first shape.
28 **e** The second shape is four of the first shape in a two by two arrangement. The orientation remains the same.
29 **b** In the second shape the sizes of the individual shapes are swapped. Large shapes become small and small shapes become large.
30 **a** In the second shape the small shape moves to the opposite end of the arrow.
31 **e** The second shape is the first shape rotated 180°.
32 **c** The second shape contains four copies of the first shape; the shape and the copies are rotated 90°, 180° and 270°. The four shapes do not touch.
33 **b** The second image is the 2D shape from the first image with the lines added to the internal corners and the additional shape(s) placed inside the 2D shape.
34 **e** The second shape has the same number of + symbols as the number of places the lines cross in the first shape.
35 **d** The second shape is made by moving the bottom section of the first shape to the top of the first shape.
36 **a** The second shape is shaded black when the first shape is shaded white.
37–42 When each shape is paired with the correct reflection, they form a single shape that is perfectly symmetrical.

37 **c**

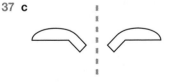

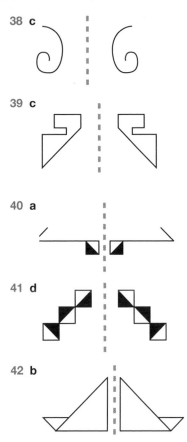

38 **c**

39 **c**

40 **a**

41 **d**

42 **b**

43 **e** The first letter represents the "handle" of the "watering can" (T has a semi-circle, U has a triangle and V has a square). The second letter represents the "spout" of the "watering can" (E has as horizontal line, F has as diagonal line and G has a vertical line).

44 **e** The first letter represents the position of the small shape on the vertical line (A has it at the bottom, B has it in the middle and C has it at the top). The second letter represents the small shape (K has a square, L has a triangle and M has a circle).

45 **c** The first letter represents the thickness of the line forming the outer rectangle (X has a thick line, Y has a medium line and Z has a thin line). The second letter represents the shape inside the rectangle (Q has an oval, R has a rhombus and S has a rectangle).

46 **b** The first letter represents the number of horizontal lines (M has two, N has three and O has four). The second letter represents the number of thicker horizontal lines with a circle at the end (F has one, G has two and H has three).

47 **e** The first letter represents the shading of the rectangle (D has black shading, E has no shading and F has grey). The second letter

represents the position of the rectangle (R has it on the left, S has it in the middle and T has it on the right).

48 **e** The first letter represents the size of the shape (J has a small shape, K has a medium shape and L has a large shape). The second letter represents the shading (F has no shading, G has horizontal lines and H has black shading).

49 **e** The head of the arrow points towards, not away from, the white face.

50 **d** The lines on the right face of this cube would be vertical if it could be made from the given net.

51 **c** The + and o symbols are in opposite positions, so they cannot be seen as adjacent faces on the cube.

52 **a** The curved edge of the "petal" shape is next to the face and therefore the point of the "petal" cannot point towards the face on the cube.

53 **c** The shading on the black and white chequerboard would be the opposite way round if this cube could be made from the given net.

54 **c** The lines on the right face of this cube would be horizontal if it could be made from the given net.

Paper 6 (pages 46–55)

1 **e** All of the options, apart from e, have an arrow made up of a solid line and an additional dashed line.

2 **c** All of the options, apart from c, have one black circle and two white circles.

3 **d** All of the shapes, apart from d, have a point at the bottom.

4 **a** All of the shapes, apart from a, are made up of five triangles.

5 **c** All of the shapes, apart from c, are made up of two black quarters, a quarter containing a white circle and a quarter containing a straight line.

6 **d** All of the shapes, apart from d, have one short line sticking out from the main shape.

7 **e** All of the shapes, apart from e, have five identical shapes that stick out from the circle.

8 **b** All of the options, apart from b, have black shading on opposite sides of the rectangles.

9 **c** All of the shapes, apart from c, have x in one corner.

10 **a** All of the options, apart from a, have matching pairs of shapes with identical shading.

11 **d** All of the shapes, apart from d, are made up of two similar shapes, one inside the other.

12 e All of the shapes, apart from e, have three circles, none of which are inside each other.

13 b The number of horizontal lines increases by one each time with the existing lines remaining in the same position.

14 a The line outside of the hexagon moves one corner clockwise each time. The black circle inside the hexagon moves one corner anticlockwise each time.

15 b One circle is removed from the top each time.

16 e The sequence alternates between a circle being added, then the new circle being attached to the other circles to form a chain.

17 c This is a repeating sequence of the shapes in the first three positions.

18 c There are two elements to this sequence. Position – the circle moves from top to middle to bottom before moving back up to middle and then top. Shading – the sequence is black, white, striped.

19 b One curved shape is added each time. Two curved shapes are added to each existing curved shape, working from left to right.

20 c One line is removed from the top and the remaining lines are shown reflected vertically each time.

21 d The sequence alternates between one and two lines being added anticlockwise to the shape each time.

22 a The shapes gain one extra side each time and the shading gets darker. The shapes remain the same size.

23 e This is a repeating sequence of the shapes in the first three positions.

24 e The short diagonal line to the left of the vertical line moves down each time. The short diagonal line to the right of the vertical line moves up each time.

25 d The second shape is the first shape reduced in size and rotated clockwise 90°.

26 e In the second shape the shading in the first shape is moved down one rectangle with the shading from the top rectangle moving to the bottom rectangle.

27 b The second shape is the shape that is a cut out "notch" from the first shape, rotated 180° (or reflected horizontally).

28 d The second shape is the two elements of the first shape joined together.

29 e The second shape is a vertical reflection of the first shape, with the shading swapped (white becomes black and black becomes white).

30 a In the second image, the small inner shape from the first image becomes the large outer shape. The outer shapes in the first image are placed inside this. The number of these shapes remains the same.

31 c The second shape is a horizontal reflection of the first shape.

32 b In the second image the shapes from the first image have been swapped in size and position.

33 a In the second image the shapes at the end of the diagonal lines have been swapped.

34 e In the second image the black and white shading has been swapped.

35 e The second shape is a 90° clockwise rotation of the first shape.

36 d The second shape shows the lines that make up the first shape, arranged horizontally one beneath the other. The length of lines remain the same length as the sides of the shape.

37 d The missing square is a horizontal reflection of the top left square.

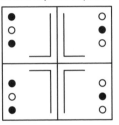

38 c The missing square is a 180° rotation of the bottom right square.

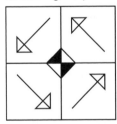

39 d The missing square contains a vertically centered square because it is in a row with vertically centered squares. The small square must be against the right-hand side of the missing square because it is in a column with small shapes against the right-hand side.

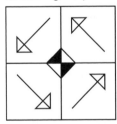

EXPANDED ANSWERS

Bond Non-Verbal Reasoning Assessment Papers 9–10 years Book 2

40 **c** The missing square contains a diagonal line matching the one on the top left square because the squares in the bottom row match the squares in the top row.

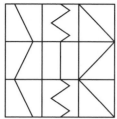

41 **b** The missing square is a vertical reflection of the square on the far right in the same row.

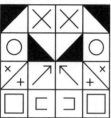

42 **e** The missing square contains three ticks because each row and column contain one of the following: one cross, two circles, three ticks and four horizontal lines.

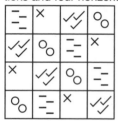

43 **e** The first letter represents the fraction the rectangle has been broken down into (G shows one whole, H shows halves and I shows thirds). The second letter represents the shading shown in one of the sections (Q has speckles, R has diagonal lines and S has black shading).

44 **a** The first letter represents the positioning of the two horizontal lines (X has them at the top and middle, Y has them at the top and bottom and Z has them at the middle and bottom). The second letter represents the shape at the bottom (D has a circle, E has a triangle and F has a square).

45 **d** The first letter represents the shape of the "bottle lid" (N has a rectangle, O has a "T" shape and P has an oval). The second letter represents the shape of the "bottle" (A has a rectangular shape, B has curved edges and C has wavy edges).

46 **e** The first letter represents the colour of the small shapes (U has white shapes, V has grey and W has black). The second letter represents the arrow direction (J has the arrow pointing up, K has it pointing down and L has it pointing up and down).

47 **c** The first letter represents the left-hand line/ shape (S has a wide rectangle, T has a narrow rectangle and U has a vertical line). The second letter represents the right-hand pattern (C has three vertical dashes, D has two vertical dashes with a black circle at the bottom and E has two vertical dashes with a black circle in the middle).

48 **a** The first letter represents the wavy lines (L has one solid wavy line, M has one solid wavy line and a dashed wavy line and N has two solid wavy lines). The second letter represents the number of short straight lines crossing the wavy lines (W has two lines, X has one line and Y has no lines).

49 **a** The L and diagonal line symbols are in opposite positions, so they cannot be seen as adjacent faces on the cube.

50 **d** The large + and x symbols are in opposite positions, so they cannot be seen as adjacent faces on the cube.

51 **a** The thick black lines are perpendicular to each other, so they cannot be parallel to each other on the cube.

52 **b** When the fully shaded black face is positioned above the smaller black square the right-hand face of the cube would have to show a horizontal line, not a fully shaded grey face.

53 **b** The straight line points towards the x symbol, so it cannot point towards the fully shaded grey face on the cube.

54 **c** The grey face and the face with the white square are in opposite positions, so they cannot be seen as adjacent faces on the cube.

53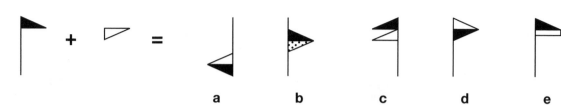

a   b   c   d   e

54

a   b   c   d   e

Paper 4

B 1   Which is the odd one out? Circle the letter.

Example

a   b   (c)   d   e

1

a   b   c   d   e

2

a   b   c   d   e

3

a   b   c   d   e

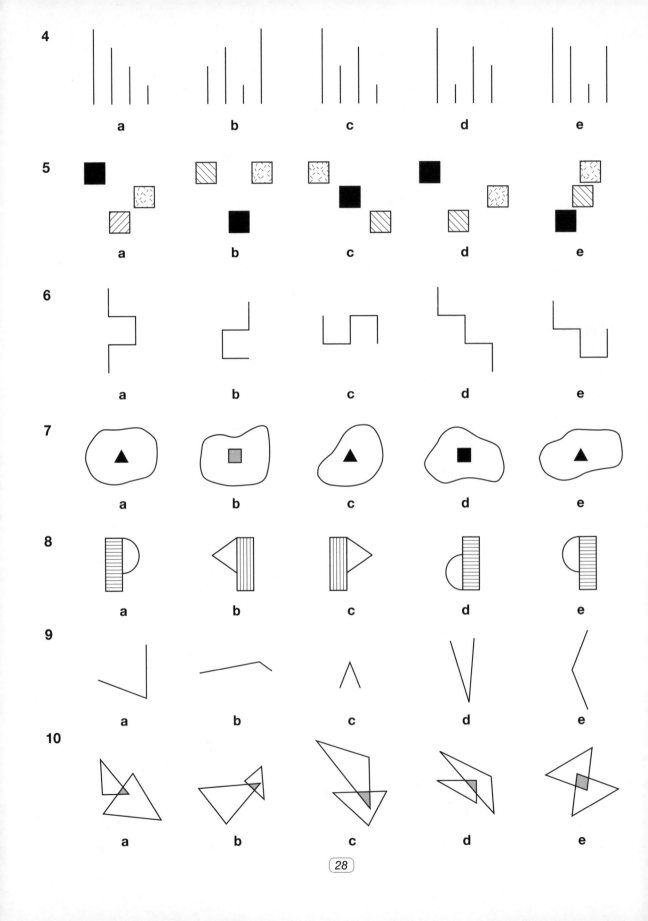

11

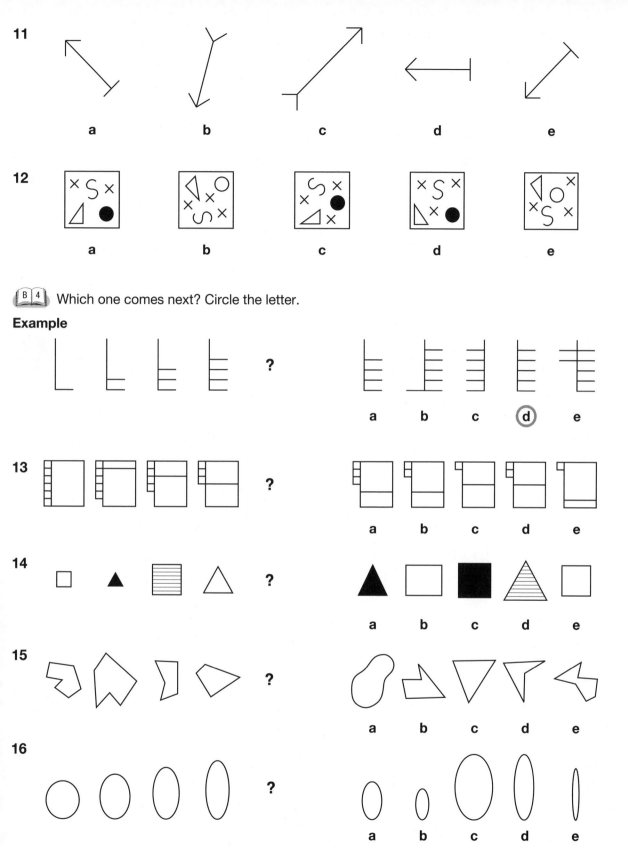

a   b   c   d   e

12

a   b   c   d   e

B 4   Which one comes next? Circle the letter.

Example

?   a   b   c   (d)   e

13   ?   a   b   c   d   e

14   ?   a   b   c   d   e

15   ?   a   b   c   d   e

16   ?   a   b   c   d   e

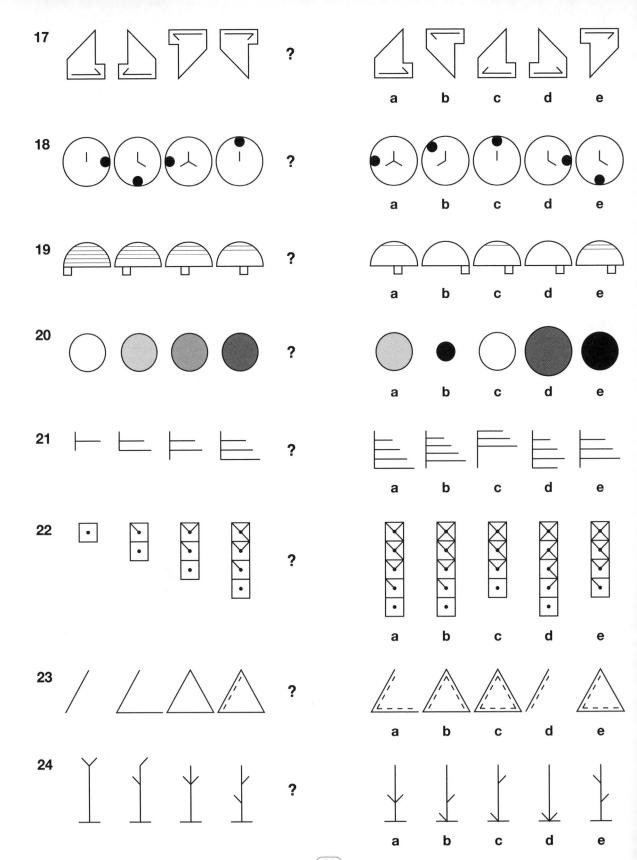

B 3 Which shape or pattern on the right completes the second pair in the same way as the first pair? Circle the letter.

Example

is to | as | is to

           a   **b**   **c**   **(d)**   **e**

25 is to | as | is to

           a   **b**   **c**   **d**   **e**

26 is to | as | is to

           a   **b**   **c**   **d**   **e**

27 is to | as | is to

           a   **b**   **c**   **d**   **e**

28 is to | as | is to

           a   **b**   **c**   **d**   **e**

29 is to | as | is to

           a   **b**   **c**   **d**   **e**

30 is to | as | is to

           a   **b**   **c**   **d**   **e**

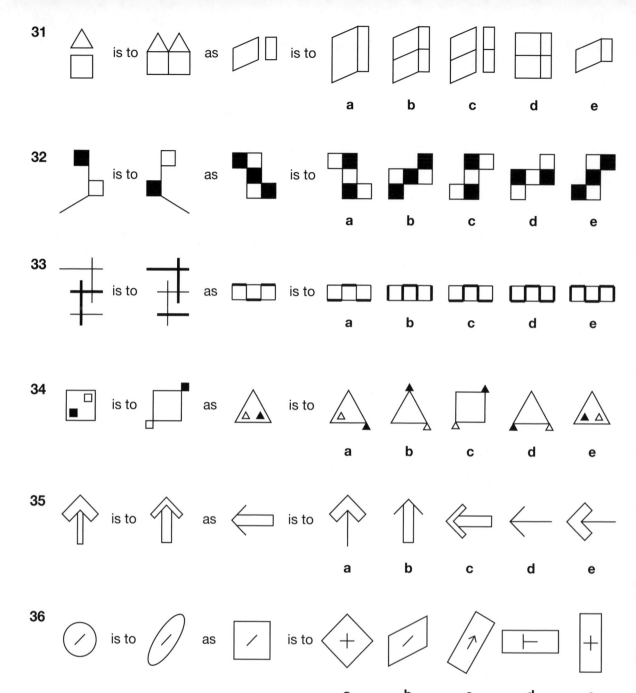

31

32

33

34

35

36

a b c d e

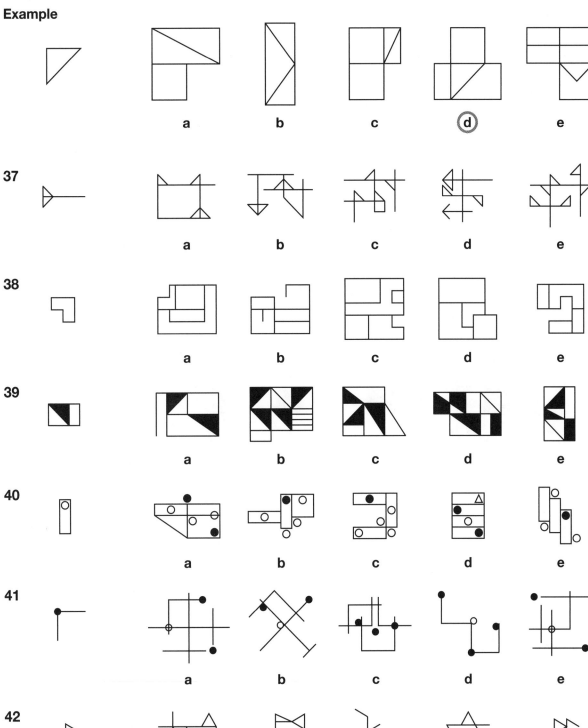

B 5 In which larger shape is the shape on the left hidden? Circle the letter.

Example

a   b   c   **d**   e

37

a   b   c   d   e

38

a   b   c   d   e

39

a   b   c   d   e

40

a   b   c   d   e

41

a   b   c   d   e

42

a   b   c   d   e

Which shape or pattern completes the larger square? Circle the letter.

Example

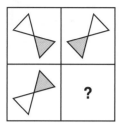

            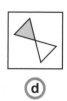

    a   b   c   d   e

43

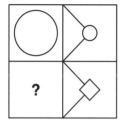

    a   b   c   d   e

44

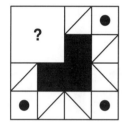

    a   b   c   d   e

45

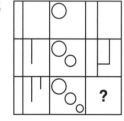

    a   b   c   d   e

46

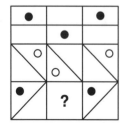

    a   b   c   d   e

47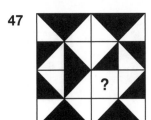

a

b

c

d

e

48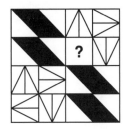

a

b

c

d

e

B 10 Which shape or pattern is made when the first two shapes or patterns are put together?
Circle the letter.

Example

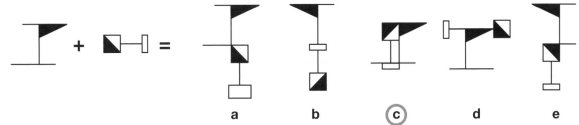

a b c d e

49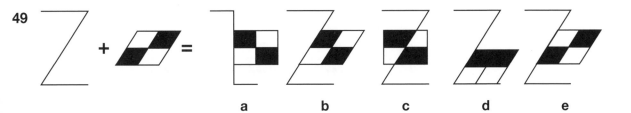

a b c d e

50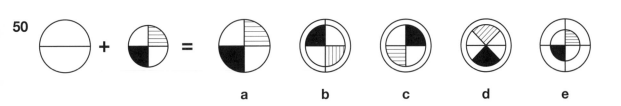

a b c d e

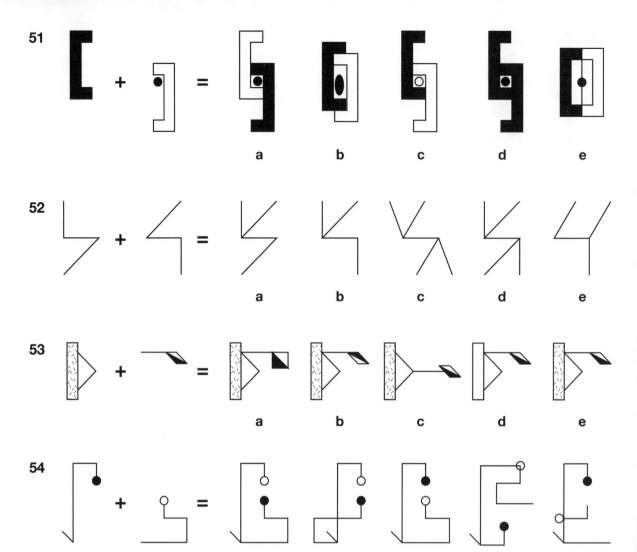

51

a   b   c   d   e

52

a   b   c   d   e

53

a   b   c   d   e

54

a   b   c   d   e

Now go to the Progress Chart to record your score!   Total   ◯   54

Paper 5

B 1 Which is the odd one out? Circle the letter.

Example

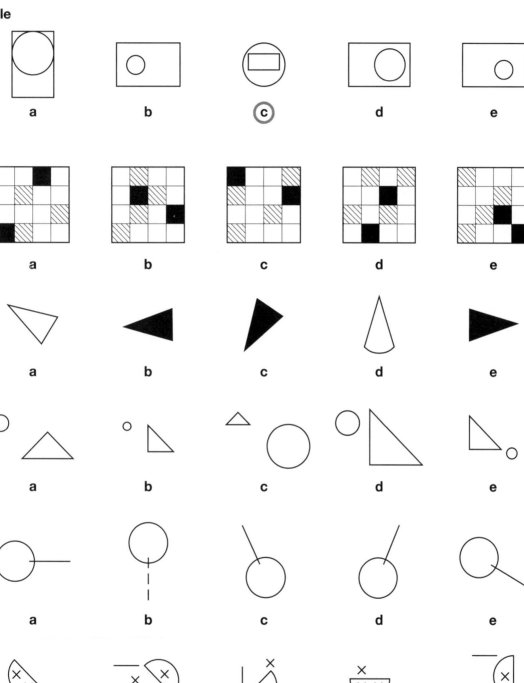

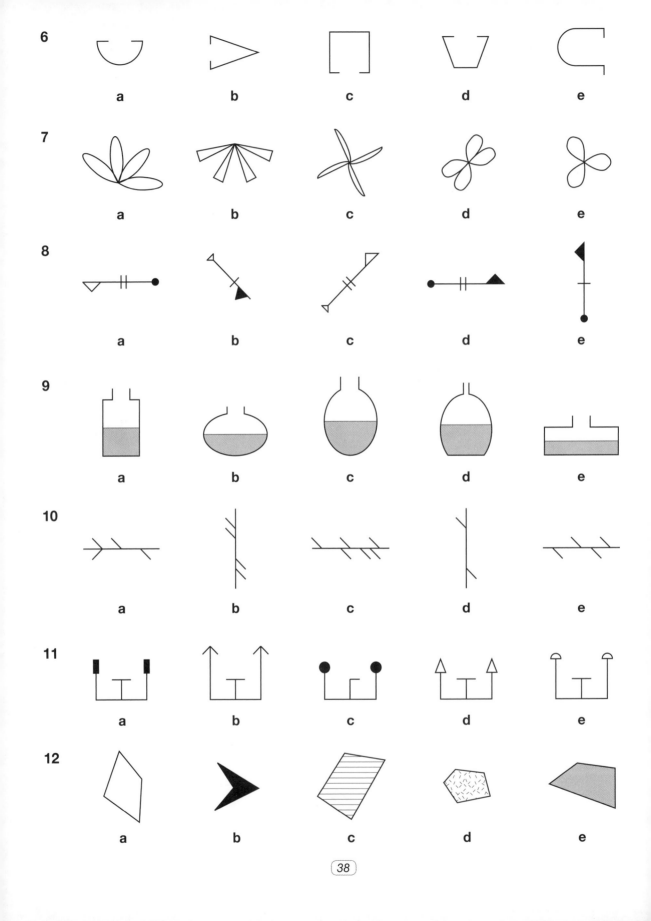

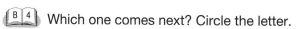 Which one comes next? Circle the letter.

Example

 ?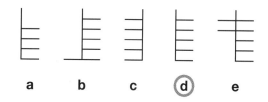

a   b   c   (d)   e

13  ?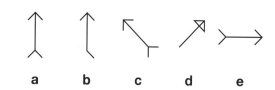

a   b   c   d   e

14 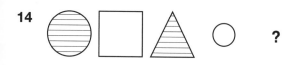 ?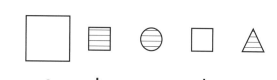

a   b   c   d   e

15  ?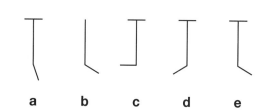

a   b   c   d   e

16  ?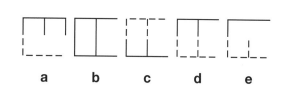

a   b   c   d   e

17 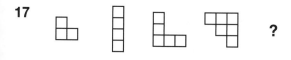 ?

a   b   c   d   e

18 ?

a   b   c   d   e

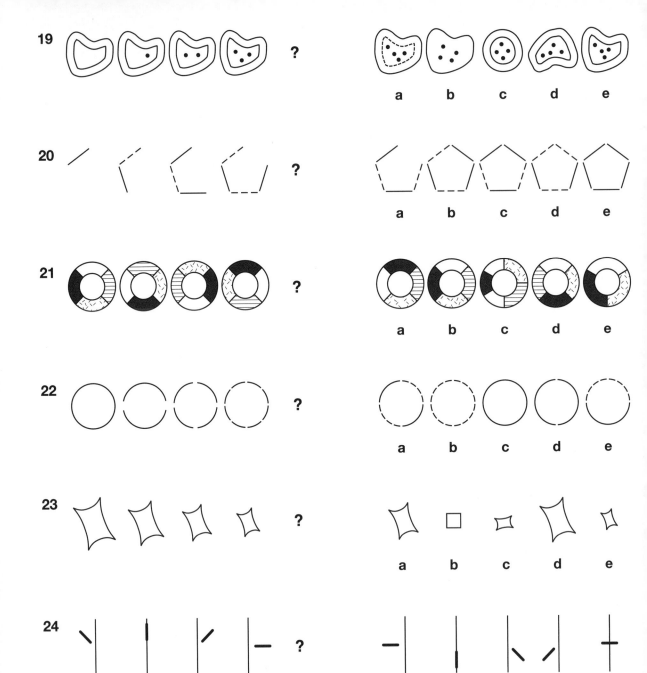

Which shape or pattern on the right completes the second pair in the same way as the first pair? Circle the letter.

Example

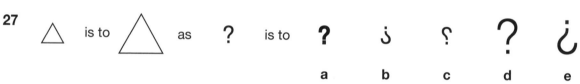

25

26

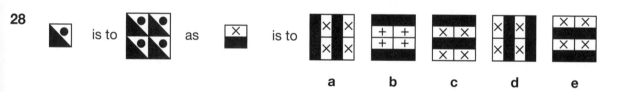

27

28

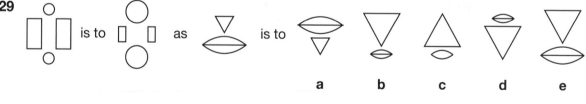

29

30

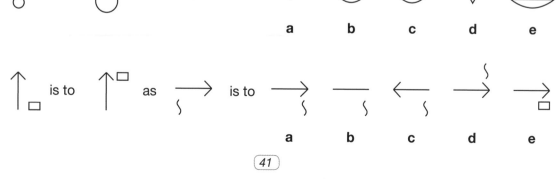

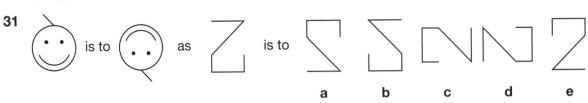

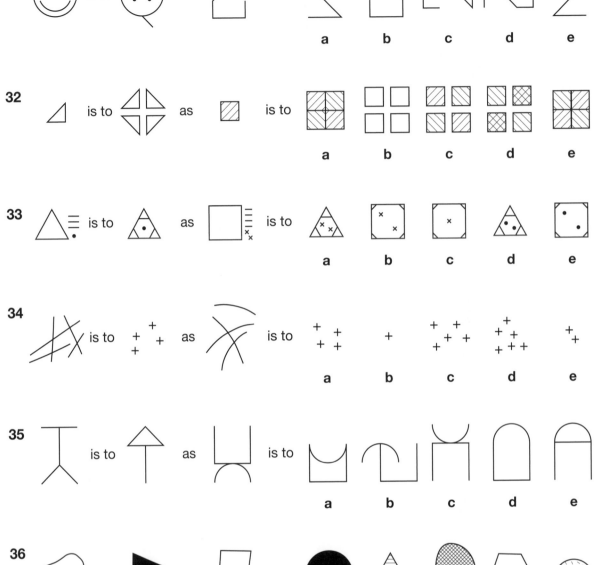

Which shape on the right is the reflection of the shape given on the left? Circle the letter.

Example

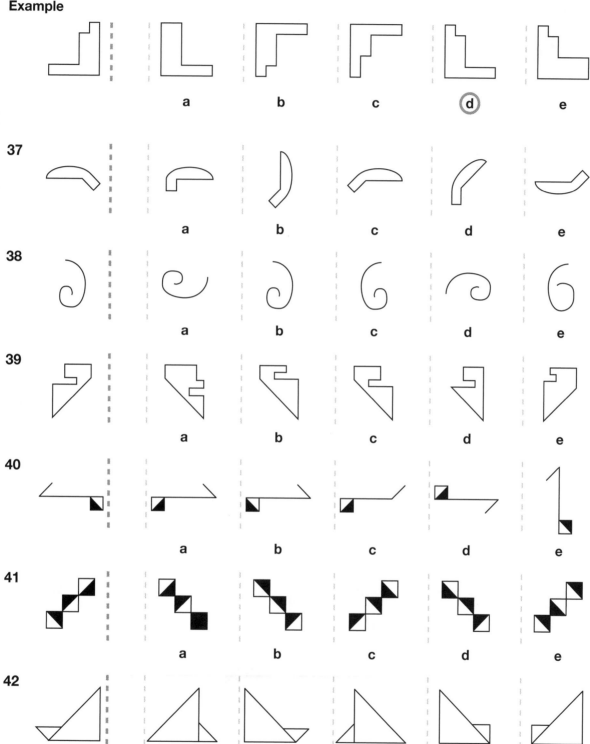

a   b   c   (d)   e

37   a   b   c   d   e

38   a   b   c   d   e

39   a   b   c   d   e

40   a   b   c   d   e

41   a   b   c   d   e

42   a   b   c   d   e

B9 Which code matches the shape or pattern given at the end of each line? Circle the letter.

Example

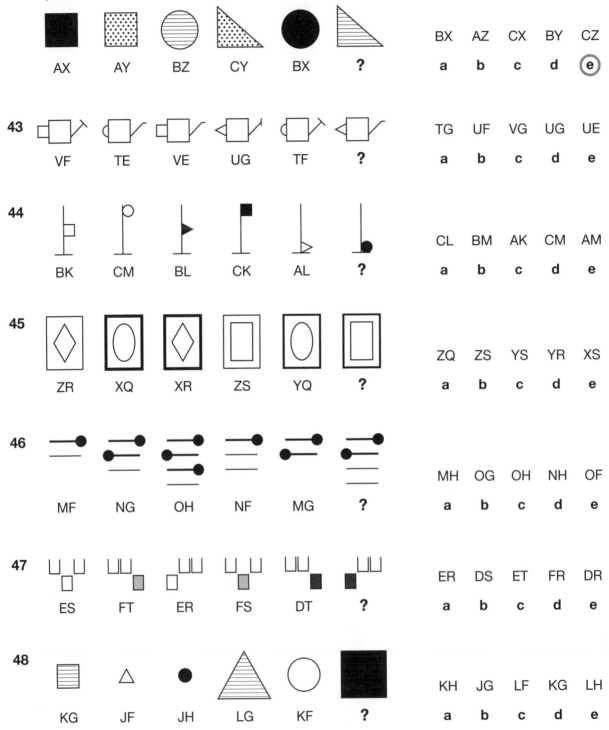

	BX	AZ	CX	BY	CZ
	a	b	c	d	(e)

43

	TG	UF	VG	UG	UE
	a	b	c	d	e

44

	CL	BM	AK	CM	AM
	a	b	c	d	e

45

	ZQ	ZS	YS	YR	XS
	a	b	c	d	e

46

	MH	OG	OH	NH	OF
	a	b	c	d	e

47

	ER	DS	ET	FR	DR
	a	b	c	d	e

48

	KH	JG	LF	KG	LH
	a	b	c	d	e

44

Which cube cannot be made from the given net? Circle the letter.

Example

a   b   c   d   e

49

a   b   c   d   e

50

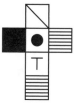

a   b   c   d   e

51

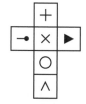

a   b   c   d   e

52

a   b   c   d   e

53

a   b   c   d   e

54

a   b   c   d   e

Paper 6

Which is the odd one out? Circle the letter.

Example

a   b   ⓒ   d   e

1

a   b   c   d   e

2

a   b   c   d   e

3

  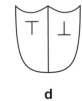 

a   b   c   d   e

4

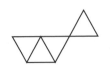   

a   b   c   d   e

5

a   b   c   d   e

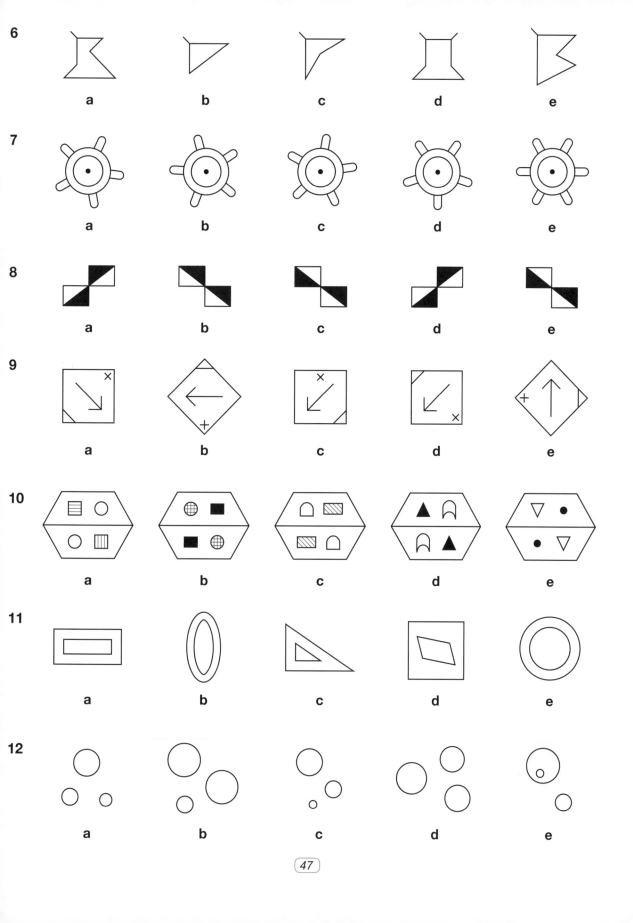

6   a   b   c   d   e

7   a   b   c   d   e

8   a   b   c   d   e

9   a   b   c   d   e

10   a   b   c   d   e

11   a   b   c   d   e

12   a   b   c   d   e

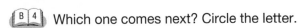 **B 4** Which one comes next? Circle the letter.

Example

 ?

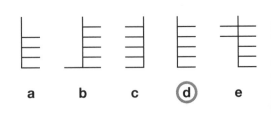

a   b   c   (d)   e

13 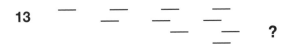 ?

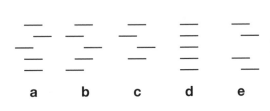

a   b   c   d   e

14 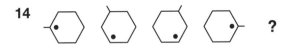 ?

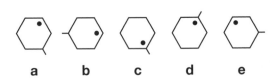

a   b   c   d   e

15  ?

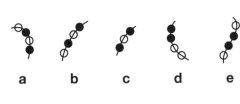

a   b   c   d   e

16  ?

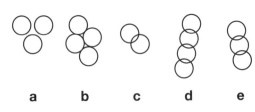

a   b   c   d   e

17 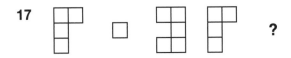 ?

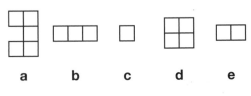

a   b   c   d   e

18 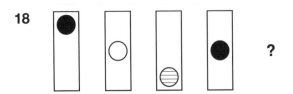 ?

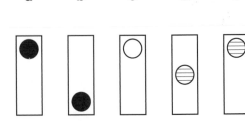

a   b   c   d   e

19  ?

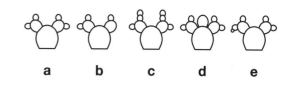

a   b   c   d   e

20 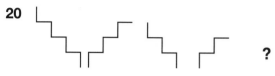 ?

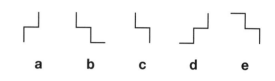

a   b   c   d   e

21  ?

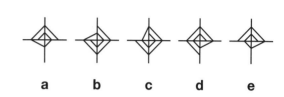

a   b   c   d   e

22  ?

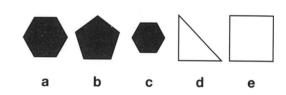

a   b   c   d   e

23 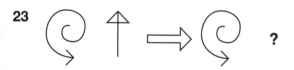 ?

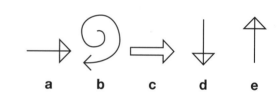

a   b   c   d   e

24  ?

a   b   c   d   e

B 3 Which shape or pattern on the right completes the second pair in the same way as the first pair? Circle the letter.

Example

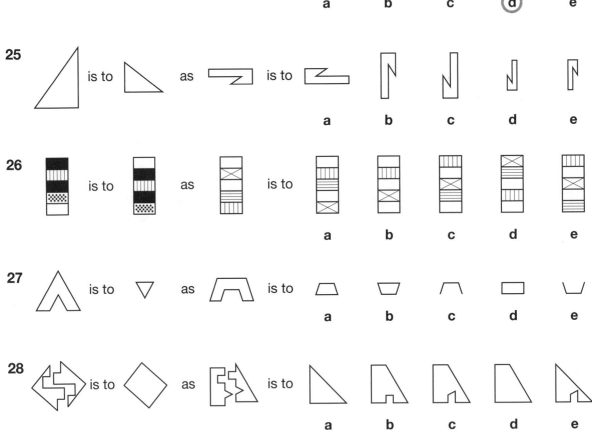

25

26

27

28

29

30

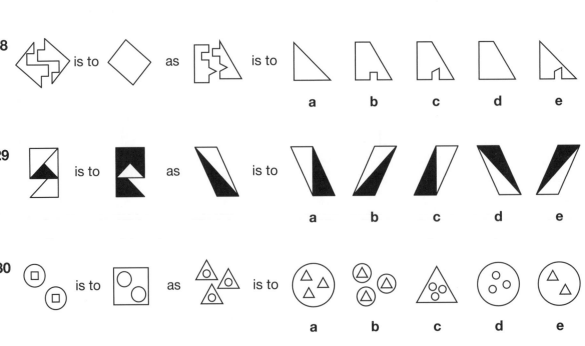

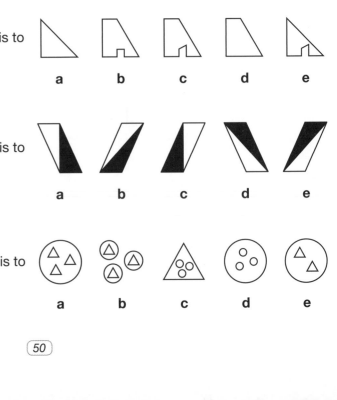

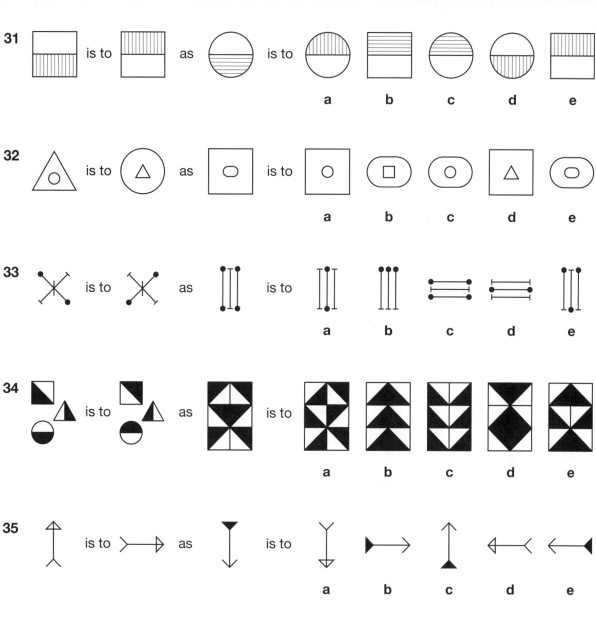

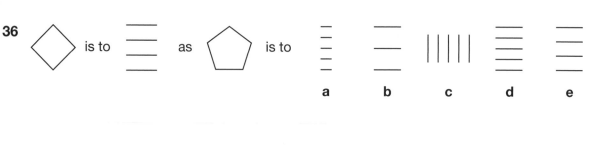

B 6 Which shape or pattern completes the larger square? Circle the letter.

Example

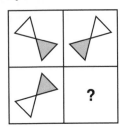

                      a   b   c   (d)   e

37

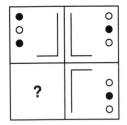

                      a   b   c   d   e

38

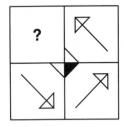

                      a   b   c   d   e

39

                      a   b   c   d   e

40

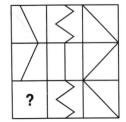

                      a   b   c   d   e

41

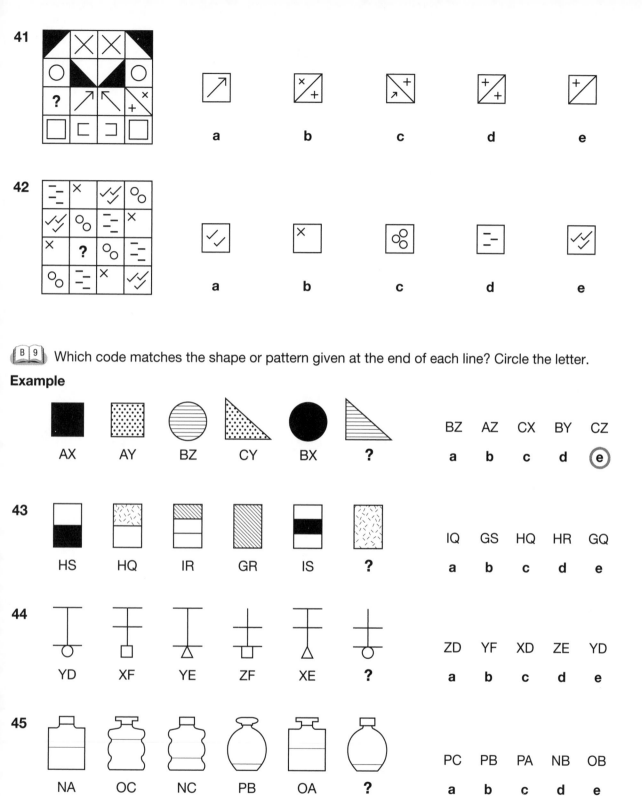

a   b   c   d   e

42

a   b   c   d   e

B 9 Which code matches the shape or pattern given at the end of each line? Circle the letter.

Example

						BZ	AZ	CX	BY	CZ
AX	AY	BZ	CY	BX	?	a	b	c	d	(e)

43

						IQ	GS	HQ	HR	GQ
HS	HQ	IR	GR	IS	?	a	b	c	d	e

44

						ZD	YF	XD	ZE	YD
YD	XF	YE	ZF	XE	?	a	b	c	d	e

45

						PC	PB	PA	NB	OB
NA	OC	NC	PB	OA	?	a	b	c	d	e

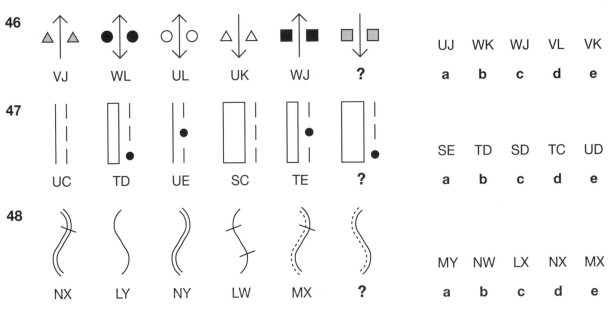

46

VJ	WL	UL	UK	WJ	?

UJ	WK	WJ	VL	VK
a	b	c	d	e

47

UC	TD	UE	SC	TE	?

SE	TD	SD	TC	UD
a	b	c	d	e

48

NX	LY	NY	LW	MX	?

MY	NW	LX	NX	MX
a	b	c	d	e

 Which cube cannot be made from the given net? Circle the letter.

Example

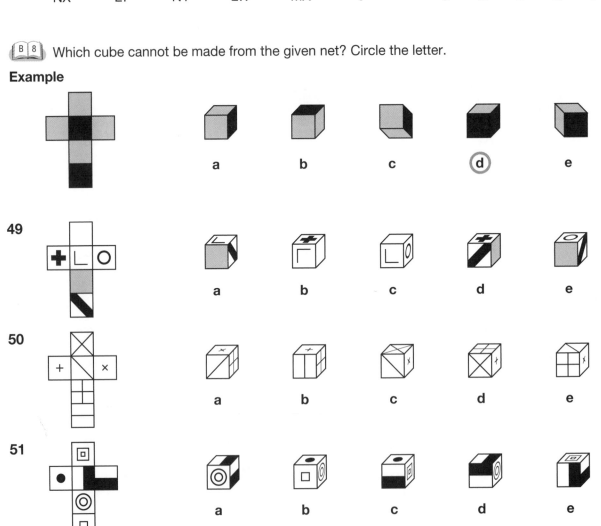

49

a b c d e

50

a b c d e

51

a b c d e

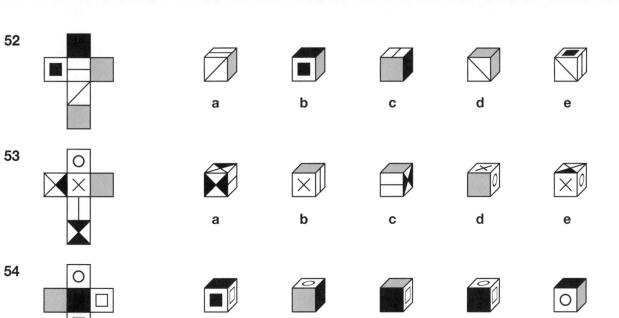

52

a   b   c   d   e

53

a   b   c   d   e

54

a   b   c   d   e

Now go to the Progress Chart to record your score!   Total ◯ 54

Progress Chart

Non-verbal Reasoning Assessment Papers 9–10 years Book 2

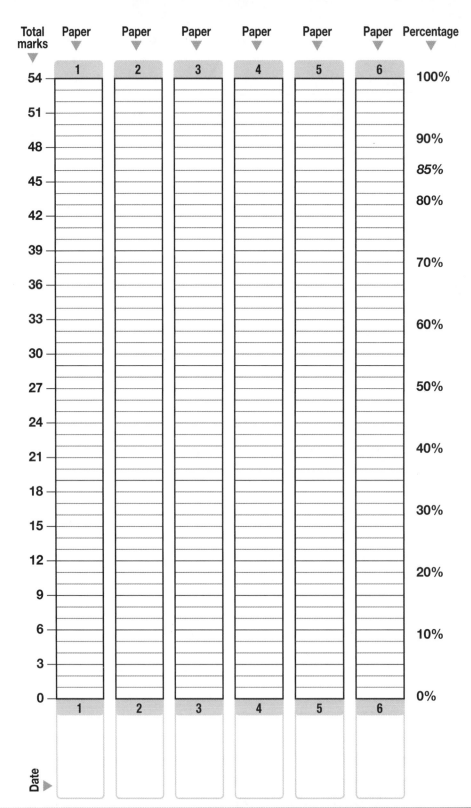

When you've finished the book use the Next Steps Planner